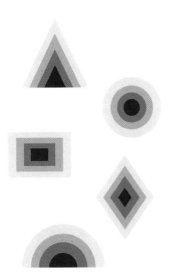

826CHI
www.826chi.org

ISBN: 1-934750-20-4

Cover and book design by Mollie Edgar

Printed in Canada

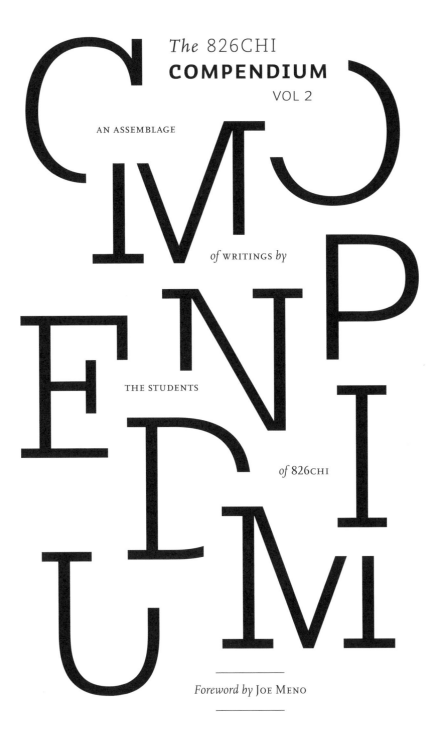

The 826CHI
COMPENDIUM
VOL 2

AN ASSEMBLAGE

of WRITINGS *by*

THE STUDENTS

of 826CHI

Foreword by JOE MENO

Contents

FIELD TRIPS

IN-SCHOOLS

AFTER-SCHOOL TUTORING *and* WRITING

AT-LARGE SUBMISSIONS

ABOUT THE STORIES AND POEMS
CONTAINED HERE WITHIN

by Joe Meno

THE PEOPLE WHO wrote them may have gotten carried away.

They may have forgotten, for the moment, themselves or their age.

They may have neglected their table manners, the periodic table of the elements, a few major historic events, several substantial math equations, the barking of a neighbor's dog. They may have gotten so swept up in their words, their ideas, the language of their poems and stories that things such as gravity no longer seemed necessary. It is for this reason that I implore you: take heed before you begin reading. The words in this volume can and will cause you to float: to suddenly ignore your taxes, or the length of the grass out back. You will find yourself untying your shoes, slipping off your black socks, and drifting up higher and higher as your head becomes something resembling a hot-air balloon. For this reason, be prepared to read this volume away from ceiling fans and all forms of commercial air traffic. There is a brilliant recklessness in these pages which those who are frightened by such things may find unsettling.

Are you faint-hearted? Please, look away.

Because the stories and poems contained here within are too fearless; they have little or no regard for doubt. Each of these is a dare. If you read them, you will be moved, as I have been, and consider doing all sorts of rash, imaginative things. You will ponder building a cuckoo clock. Or opening a record store. Or buying a burrow owl. You will forget all the reasons against such things and you, yourself, will get carried away, too.

As the great poet Charles Baudelaire once noted, "Curiosity may be the starting point for genius." In writing these stories, these poems, these essays, the authors included in this second compendium of writing produced at 826CHI, a non-profit writing and tutoring center, did one of the bravest things a thinking person can do, and that is to use their curiosity, their improbable imaginations, to conjure up something that did not exist before, something altogether new. I believe this is the highest calling any of us can aspire to, and time and time again in this book, these writers, who just so happen to be young, write with an abandon and inventiveness that is nothing short of startling.

For some of us, it may be necessary to be so startled.

Here within this indelible volume, you will find many different kinds of writings: a story about a boy in love with a tree and an essay about the importance of pad thai. There is the story of Bob the panda-pig who lives in the woods behind Burger King, and another about a volcano in Kentucky. You will read about a vampire who drinks bleach while watching too much television, and also about the last piece of untouched land on earth.

In their brevity, with their humor, and with their inimitable explosions of imagination, these stories and poems and pieces of creative non-fiction not only remind us why storytelling is so important, but they are also evidence that these young writers—ignoring other, more obvious forms of enjoyment and expression—are authoring their own futures, constructing a universe of endless possibilities. This feels important. This feels big. This feels exciting. This feels like the world as we know isn't ending; but developing in new, unpredictable ways. Reading this second compendium of 826CHI stories, it's impossible not to notice the vitality of language, the unadulterated bursts of discovery, so that, in the end, it reminds us of what a few well-chosen sentences can do, how entire lives can be altered by the right word.

Do not take these words, these stories, these poems lightly. They are a little too interesting, a little too drastic to be ignored. In them, we can identify the best parts of ourselves, and all of our best reasons to hope.

WORKSHOPS

826CHI offers workshops in the evenings and on the weekends throughout the school year, and more summer workshops than you can shake a popsicle stick at. Over the course of the year, this adds up to nearly one hundred different classes for students to choose from, each culminating in new writing and a variety of creative projects.

Students can sign up for workshops exploring traditional forms of writing such as short fiction and poetry, as well as offbeat classes like Zombies Can't Write (But Kids Can!), Talking Trash: Inspiration Through Everyday Artifacts, and The Art of the Circus. The aim of all of our workshops is to expose students to a variety of new art and writing, and to help them cultivate their writing skills. Equally important? Making writing fun.

The workshops featured in this book represent only a handful of the many offered year-round at 826CHI. Love a good backstory? Descriptions for these particular workshops are located at the end of this book.

David Calloway Interviews an Eagle

BY David Calloway, Jr., *Grade 4*
FROM *Newsbreak Breakout!, Fall 2009*

I'm conducting this interview on top of a mountain and I'm scared
out of my pants. It's worth it, though. Today, I am speaking to the
one and only—the guy you see on a quarter—Bob the Eagle.

David Calloway: Do you like soaring through the sky?
[Laughs.]

Bob the Eagle: Of course. Sometimes I even see you playing.

DC: Is it hard swooping down from the sky and catching prey?

BE: It's pretty hard. It takes a lot of energy.

DC: How does it feel to touch clouds?

BE: It feels good. The clouds feel like cotton candy.

DC: What is a personal goal for you?

BE: Well, one of my goals is to catch 1,000 fish this year.

DC: Do you like music?

BE: I like air hop. It's the new version of hip hop.

DC: Is it cool being on flags and quarters?

BE: It's awesome! Everyone knows me.

DC: What's your favorite food?

BE: When no one is watching, I secretly make cheeseburgers.

DC: Finally, how does it feel when states and buildings are taking your spot on quarters?

BE: It's horrible. I was there first.

A Taste of My Family

BY Alex Lundsgaarde, *Grade 5*
FROM *A 'Whole' Lot of Food and Memoir Writing, Fall 2009*

PAD THAI IS A big part of my family's history. From the scorching hot southern parts of Thailand to here, in the Windy City.

Life was rough for my grandparents. They didn't have much of anything. When they grew older, they sought out an education, and moved to the United States. Here, they met and got married. Then came my mother, aunt, and uncle.

When my mom was about my age, she would sit by my grandma whenever she cooked. My mom would observe every single spice and ingredient my grandma put into her recipes. Now that my mom's older, I do the same.

When my mom makes pad thai, I can hear her chopping fresh tofu in the kitchen. The rice noodles go in the frying pan with some garlic, the sizzling like music to my ears.

I know that something delicious is about to be made. As soon as the sweet tamarind aroma fills the air, I am almost falling off my chair.

It's an amazing sensation as I take the first bite. The lime and tamarind mixed together is like a colorful, eye-popping fireworks show. The noodles, fried until they are golden, are bursting with flavor. As steam from the dish rolls up my face, I think of Thailand. I think of my grandparents. The thought of it makes me feel safe and warm.

My mom inspires me to try new things with her cooking. I hope that someday I'll be able to inspire someone somewhere in the world with something I do well.

Rimbaud

BY Zeta Moore, *Grade 11*
FROM *Young Writers Camp with Local Authors, Summer 2009*

I am lost

I am immortal

I am the result of a pile of mistakes

I am too young to know what is good for me and too old to
lie in a crib and cry until my breaths are shot for Mama

Nobody knows I am the king of France

I am a slave to my thoughts and write them in streams and
rip them apart

I want to crucify people with these thoughts if they want to be crucified

I am trying to run from myself, and I think that if I run far enough, I won't know who I am

So my thoughts will be someone else's

And I will be a shell.

The Only Modern Nonfiction Castle-and-Dragon Tale

BY Matthew Schumm, *Grade 7*
FROM *I Was a Teenage Zine Fiend, Fall 2009*

PART I: THE WOMAN

Paul P. Pentitius purposefully crossed the threshold of his suburban house. He had wire rimmed spectacles, thinning hair, and a slight, unassuming build. He got into his nondescript sedan and drove his way over to the office.

Paul was your average bachelor office worker. Every morning, he got into the suit and tie he would eventually be buried in, drove over to Starbucks, got a coffee and sandwich, and then went over to the office, where he worked for a brokerage firm. He then came home, ate a feast of Ramen, and went to bed.

He was forty years old.

And it never occurred to him that he was wasting his life.

After looking at some colorful graphs, talking to equally colorful (though in language, rather than the visual sense) investors, and generally doing boring stuff, he got a call shortly before he would have left the office.

"Hello, sir. How may I help you?" he inquired.

"I'm a woman."

Uh-oh. The caller had an impatient tone. Paul sensed a high-powered executive. He could practically hear her fingers drumming on her desk.

"So sorry, madam," he said in an oily voice. "If there is anything—"

"Shut up!" said the executive. "What's your policy on selling stock for a newly created company?"

"Erm, you could do it, but I don't think anyone would buy it—"

"Meet me at the library at seven thirty to discuss this, Mr. Pentitius."

"But, madam, it's seven fifteen."

"Then go!"

And she hung up.

Paul rushed down to his car, and drove at high speed to the library. He parked at a meter and walked inside.

He hadn't been in the library for a very long time. He passed the children's section as he walked upstairs. Waiting for him at one of the desks was a tall woman in a severe suit and tie with her black hair pulled up in a tight bun. Just as Paul had imagined her.

"I presume you're Mr. Pentitius?" she asked.

"That's me," he confirmed as he slid onto a chair across the table from her.

"Listen," she said. "I have an operation in Idaho with the foresting industry. We are sending in woodcutters in a few weeks. We have a giant plot of forested land we are going to completely rip up. Are you telling me we can't sell stock now?"

"I—"

"Listen, get it done, alright?" she said and flounced off, her heels clicking as she strode over to the elevator and jabbed at a button. The elevator doors slid open and she vanished from sight.

Paul slowly made his way out the library doors. As he passed the children's section, he saw a poster about banned books. He stopped to look.

The poster mentioned a children's book called *The Lorax*. It was about a little tree creature that had gotten bullied by creatures called Once-lers into letting them cut down all the trees. The poster complained that the book had been banned because it "criminalized the foresting industry."

As he read the poster, Paul realized how ridiculous it was to ban a book like this. He also realized how wrong the executive was. He had to try and stop this company from ripping up trees in Idaho.

But how would he do it?

Two months, later, Paul sat at his desk and opened his e-mail. A bubble popped up, telling him he had one new message. When Paul saw what it was, he almost danced for joy.

Linda Arbor-Mortis, CEO of the new developing company Arbor-Mortis Land Developers, had been arrested for attempting to develop on an endangered caribou habitat in Idaho. If it had not been for Paul finding a way to stop her, it is likely that the illegality of Linda's actions would not have been exposed before she had the forest cut down.

Fresh off his victory in Idaho, Paul decided to start a non-profit organization called the Arborvita Association. The first grant that Paul submitted was to ask for money to fund a Save the Trees Seminar, where representatives from logging companies would meet and discuss eco-friendly ways to obtain wood.

The e-mail read:

Dear Mr. Pentitius,
We have considered your proposal and are willing to grant you $4,000 dollars to fund your organization's Save the Trees Seminar.

Sincerely,
Ann DeMalia, Foundation for the Preservation of Wildlife

THE END

(OR IS IT A NEW BEGINNING?)

Haiku

BY Abigail Africa, *Grade 5/6*
FROM *Salt Water + You = Art Making + Haiku, Spring 2009*

Beautiful music—
a pretty, tiny, green bird,
wings flapping me, leaves.

Splatters of purple—
orange, and shades of pale green.
A word that's quite odd.

A flash of purple
fading into the distance—
stream of violet.

Colored explosion:
square petals disconnected—
unfitting outline.

Haiku

Zola Price, *Grade 4*
FROM *Salt Water + You = Art Making + Haiku, Spring 2009*

32 Monkeys swing through trees.
Their fur ripples. As they climb,
the juice of fruit drips.

Haiku

BY Cherokee John Paul Sperry, *Grade 4*
FROM *Salt Water + You = Art Making + Haiku, Spring 2009*

A frog and a pond.   33
A frog jumps in the pond—*splash*.
No frog and no pond.

What is a green tree?
Is it cornmeal and water?
No, that is cornbread.

The Goddess and the Cobra

BY Hannah Barlow, *Grade 5*
FROM *Sir Downward Dog and the Goddess of Cobraland Unite Under a Dancing Half-Moon: Yoga! Storytelling! Illustrating!, Fall 2009*

34 THE GODDESS WAS a beautiful woman who lived on a hill. She was dedicated to the trees in the village. She would stretch her arms across the forest and protect the Monkeys and the Locusts and the Eagles who settled in the branches of the great trees. The Monkeys were so thankful for the Goddess that they gathered bunches of bananas and gave them to her. It was their entire year's supply. But the Goddess was not greedy, so she kindly declined. The Locusts were so grateful they said that they would give up their wings so she could soar up to the heavens where she belonged. The Goddess smiled and asked what the poor Locusts would do without their wings. The Eagles were so thankful that they asked if they could build her a wondrous nest. The Goddess said, "If the nest was the size of me, you could be building it forever. I don't want you to waste your life."

So, things continued normally until the Cobra arrived. He slithered into the great forest and cleared a large spot to nest. The Goddess greeted him and took his hand kindly in her soft, russet palm. Her eyes were an eccentric green and her hair a calm terra cotta falling over her perfectly-composed face. She instructed the Monkeys and the Locusts and the Eagles to help the Cobra to assemble a nest. The Monkeys and the Locusts and the Eagles worked hard and long, while the Cobra was "away". He felt a bit sorry that the animals in the forest were working so hard when soon he would pierce their hearts with evil and dread.

The Cobra shook his feelings off in a half-second. His job was to betray, to deceive. He fixed his yellow eyes on the Warrior and the Archer, two inseparable brothers. They looked content—oblivious to what was to happen. The Cobra sent the Archer to the other side of the valley and ordered him to send an arrow across, reassured his brother would be out of the way. Of course, the Cobra knew this was untrue.

The Archer ran, with great speed, to the other side. He counted to five, then pulled a sharp, red-tipped arrow and launched it across. He saw a staggering figure on the other side, but ignored it because his eyes could not see clearly.

Across the valley, a sharp, red-tipped arrow pierced through the Warrior's chest. He gasped for air, then fell to the rocky ground, clutching his chest. The Cobra watched the scene with his keen yellow eyes. Another half-second of

The Goddess watched the red-tipped arrow fly barely over her head. She quickly turned her head, her terra cotta hair flying to the side. She watched as the arrow plunged through the Warrior's chest. She gasped as she saw the Cobra watching nearby. That was when she knew—she knew everything.

With one step, the Goddess climbed up to the mountain. She picked up the Warrior. She healed him with a soft touch, reuniting him with his brother. But then, the Cobra gave the Archer and the Warrior a swift tail flick. They nodded and began to shoot below. The Monkeys and the Locusts and the Eagles screeched in horror. All the hard work, all the kindness they had given the world, and this is what they received. The Cobra's yellow eyes, with slits for pupils, widened. With another tail flick, the brothers began to fight each other. The animals were screeching and clawing.

The Goddess looked around at the destruction. Her beautiful green eyes were almost welling up with tears. She picked the animals up in one hand, and the Archer, the Warrior, and the Cobra in the other.

"Brothers," she spoke softly.

She addressed the Archer and the Warrior. "You two were inseparable. You loved each other to the ends of the earth. Look what he has done to you."

"You," she looked at the Cobra with sorrowful eyes. "Look what you have done to such a peaceful place. A place of happiness."

With that, the Goddess let the others down, and threw the Cobra up into the air, throwing all the world's greed and violence with him. Because of this, the little forest up in the hills will always be peaceful and happy.

The Cardboard Adventures of Paper Face Buck

BY Benito Delgadillo, Jerod Lockhart, and Melody Trinh,
Grade 7, Grade 5, and Grade 7
FROM *Middle School Writing Camp II, Summer 2009*

38 THE CITY OF STAPLETOWN, when viewed from high above, looked like a giant stapler. In downtown Stapletown lived a boy named Buck who had a face made of brown cardboard paper. Some people called him Paper Face Buck. On each side of his head he wore a different expression—in the front, he was happy; in the back, he looked sad; on the right side, his face was scared; and on the left, his face was angry. And if you were taller than Buck, you would see the confused face on top.

Buck lived with his grandmother, Jalen, who was a regular old person for the most part, except that when she put magical tissue in her pockets she could fly.

There also lived in Stapletown a Hochififibot, which was a giant creature made from a horse, a chicken, a firefighter, and a robot. He was incredibly annoying because he always went around telling corny jokes and spraying people from his firehose hooves.

One day, Paper Face Buck and Jalen were walking to the park to play football with Sombrero Steve, Lasso Larry, and Alex van Goobers. All of a sudden, the Hochififibot jumped in front of them.

"Why couldn't the first grader get into the pirate movie?" clucked the Hochififibot.

"Why?" yelled Jalen and Paper Face Buck.

"Because it was rated *arrrrrgggh*!"

Jalen and Paper Face Buck did not laugh, so the Hochififibot sprayed them both with water and galloped away.

Suddenly, Paper Face Buck's cardboard faces began to droop. He was soaked like a goldfish and he no longer had lips to speak. His face was melting away!

Grandma Jalen stuffed her magic tissue in her pockets and flew after the Hochififibot. When she was directly above him, she dropped a football on him, giving him a giant *clonk* on his head. The Hochififibot got dizzy and fell down.

"Can't you see what you've done to this poor child?" asked Grandma Jalen.

"I'm terribly sorry," said the Hochififibot. "That football on the head must have restored my common sense. Let's go fix this!"

Grandma Jalen and the Hochififibot went to the radioactive store and bought a box made of platinum and rubies.

39

They took it back to Buck who was sitting on a park bench, feeling terribly sad as he melted away.

"Don't be sad!" cried the Hochififibot. With that, Grandma Jalen and the Hochififibot pulled out the radioactive box made of platinum and rubies.

"This will be your new head," said Grandma Jalen. Buck was extremely happy.

From that day on, things were just fine in Stapletown, and the Hochififibot told only funny jokes!

The Name

BY Alexander Rakov, *Grade 6*
FROM *Poemography, Fall 2009*

As I walk down the street, I see
a piece of paper floating in the air.
As I catch it, I see a name.
It is my own name, sprawled
carelessly on the paper.
I am known.

Frisbees of Miraculous Flavor

BY Milo Carpenter, *Grade 4*
FROM *A 'Whole' Lot of Food and Memoir Writing, Fall 2009*

MY FAMILY LOVES PIZZA. My sister, my mom, me, and my short-haired, green-eyed dad. But, for a long time, we didn't really make it. We just bought it at pizza shops.

My dad wanted to make his own pizza and calzones—calzones are just rolled-up pizzas. He wanted to make them in our kitchen, which has a stove with a built-in cutting board next to it, a huge counter on the wall, and in the middle, a table with no legs. Inside the table is our dishwasher, and on the ceiling are hanging pots and pans.

My dad's pizzas are like frisbees of miraculous flavor. The smell of them makes me so hungry because I really want to eat it! They are one of the most amazing things that a man who loves black shirts and whose name is Richard, but is called Dick, can make.

Mi Cultura

BY Reina Delgado, *Grade 12*
FROM *I Was a Teenage Zine Fiend, Fall 2009*

When I see myself in the mirror I know there is more
than what I see. I symbolize
my culture.
You put up a wall, you think that is going to keep me away.
¡No!
My Culture—
        I eat a delicious *enchilada* that *mi mamita* makes in the
morning,
from a recipe passed on from *mi abuelita*.
My Culture—
        My parents, who had faith when coming to the US
for a better life
        and education for their children's generation.
After, you discriminated against me.
After, you made me feel less.

After, you made me frown.

But don't count on victory, don't count on me to make you rich.

My Culture—

Every day, facing hard labor, complicated paperwork, and family separation.

Because I work at a job that no one wants.

Because I accept leftovers.

My Culture—

It is something I always think about.

Since the beginning of *mi escritura*

yo regreso a mi cultura.

Flying

BY Katie Farr, *Grade 2*
FROM *Elementary Writing Camp I, Summer 2009*

Emily Dickinson

45

catching birds

in the afternoon

out in the backyard

because she is having fun.

The Cat

BY Gabrielle Roberts, *Grade 2*
FROM *Elementary Writing Camp I, Summer 2009*

46   The good cat
wanders to New York
at 8:30PM
from Mexico
to go to the University.

Isabell

BY Phoebe Murtagh, *Grade 8*
FROM *I Was a Teenage Zine Fiend, 2009*

ISABELL PULLED HER LEGS CLOSER to her body. She was curled into a giant armchair in her almost-favorite hangout: a used bookstore on the north side where no one cared if you read, bought, or burned dictionaries in the bathroom. She held a Jane Austen novel in one hand, and a badly-made decaf latte in the other. Isabell sipped slowly at the latte, making a mental note to add an extra pack of raw sugar and half a cup of water if she wanted to survive until her mother came and got her.

Isabell tapped her foot along to whatever was playing on the front computer, wondering in the back of her head whose iTunes list it was. Nearby, some kid was telling a friend about something that had happened to a hamster a few days earlier.

"...and he ate it *all*!"

The friend muttered something inaudible, causing the girl to exclaim, "That, too!"

Isabell tried to block out the chatter and focus on her page.

"And the other hamster thinks he's a cat!"

"Yeah, sure."

"Seriously!"

Pondering the possibility of a hamster-cat identity crisis, Isabell's eyes fell on a pale girl with flat blonde hair reading a hardcover copy of *Twilight*. As she turned the page, the girl's green eyes expanded and she let out a squeak. Despite her excitement, something about her made Isabell wonder if it wasn't the girl's fifth time reading the words before her. The girl squeaked again, and pulled out a cell phone, punching in two numbers, then hitting CALL. Isabell's sharp ears picked up the girl's words.

"C? Hi, it's A. I just finished the last chapter, and I'm going to read the next one... Oh, okay. T.T.U.L. Bye." She hung up the phone and put it in her backpack.

Isabell's attention was turned to her book when she heard, "Um, excuse me."

The green-eyed girl was standing over her, now holding a paperback copy of *New Moon*.

"My name's Amy."

"I'm Isabell. Hi."

"Hi. I was just wondering what you were reading," said Amy.

"*Persuasion* by Jane Austen. You're reading *New Moon*?"

"Yes. Or, I'm about to start. That's what I was hoping you could help me with. My friend Courtney is away, and she and I normally read books together, and I was wondering if you would like to read with me."

Isabell hesitated. "Do I have to read *New Moon*?" she asked.

"I guess not... wouldn't you want to?"

"No, I don't have a very high opinion of the *Twilight* books," Isabell told her.

"Oh. What didn't you like about it?" asked Amy.

"I haven't read it," said Isabell, "but I'm tired of hearing how it's the best book ever."

"Well, if you didn't read it, how do you know you don't like it?"

"I don't. I'll probably read it sometime, but not for a while." Isabell thought for a moment. "What do you like about it?"

"Reading it with my friends," answered Amy automatically.

"Your friend, Courtney—is her last name Ramone?"

"No, it's Chatwind. She's on vacation. She really likes all of the *Twilight* books. She's the one who told me about them in the first place. They're her favorites."

"I like the *Harry Potter* series," said Isabell.

"Me, too," said Amy.

"Does Courtney?"

Amy looked down and began fiddling with her sleeve.

"No," she answered. "She doesn't like them much anymore."

"What else doesn't Courtney like any more?" asked Isabell, narrowing her eyes thoughtfully.

"Teddy bears, weirdness, making up new games..." Amy grew quiet.

"How old are you, Amy?" asked Isabell.

"Thirteen and a half."

"Me, too," said Isabell. "Do you and Courtney go to the same school?"

"No," Amy said shortly. "Courtney's a half-year older than me, so she's in high school." Isabell noticed how Amy seemed to want to avoid talking about her friend.

"How long have you and she been friends?"

"Forever," said Amy.

"But now that she's older, she doesn't like the same stuff as you?" asked Isabell.

"We like some of the same things," defended Amy. "But, it's just a bit harder than it used to be. And sometimes I get scared we can't still be friends."

"I think you still can be," Isabell ventured.

"I hope so." Amy smiled. "You should be a psychologist when you grow up! You're really good at it."

Isabell laughed. "Maybe I will be."

Amy's phone rang, interrupting the girls. She took the call.

"It's my mom. She's coming to pick me up." Amy got to her feet. "Thanks, Isabell. You really made me feel better."

Isabell smiled as Amy ran off. She tried to ignore the chatter behind her as she turned back to her book.

The Key

BY Jack Sullivan, *Grade 10*
FROM *Young Writers Camp with Local Authors, Summer 2009*

52

It's a key
    a rusty dirty brown old
key

and yet the more I think about it
the more I focus all my mental energy on it
something happens
I'm not where I was
                before
I'm somewhere else
with the key
    and before me is
    a door
    a red door and I take
    the crappy key and I stick it in

turn and open
    and suddenly
I'm somewhere else
I'm with

Melissa and
Connor
and Karen
and we are working
    somewhere

and it gets late and we have nowhere to go so
we go to Karen's
at some insane hour in the morning
with demonic cousins
nymphet sister
    and parents
who know no English
and we sit there
her fluorescent kitchen
and non-light of the full moon
bathing us
    in glorious nothing
and we watch crappy movies
    and drink too much Red Bull
and flirt in ways
that would annoy even our peers

I am asleep
    on the couch
thinking of her
she's away

holding the key
the key
    the key to life and memory and my cerebral
    cortex
and then it's morning
hastily spoken Spanish
and pancakes with chocolate syrup
Melissa kisses me before I leave
    and I burst into flames and stick the key in the door
and suddenly
I'm not where I was before
    but where I always was
    sitting here
with that ratty old key
the key to memory
    to thought
to life
and once again
just to remind you
    or me
or whomever this
    may concern

Teaching Rod Blagojevich How to Eat Chocolate

BY Matthew Schumm, *Grade 7*
FROM *Travel the World Through Chocolate, Spring 2009*

"HERE," I SAID, handing the disgruntled ex-governor a piece of chocolate.

"Why should I eat chocolate?! I don't have time for this!" he growled, red in the face.

"Trust me, you'll like it," was my reply. I shoved it closer to the criminal politico's mouth. "Smell it," I ordered.

He glared at me, but sniffed it all the same. Then, shockingly, he broke into a grin.

"Bitter. Shady. Smells like money. Ohh, money," he said, practically smothering his nose with the square of cocoa. I grinned. This was so funny. I wanted to teach a kleptomaniac how to eat chocolate every day.

"Now touch it," I commanded.

He rubbed it tenderly.

"It should feel smooth," I said.

"Smooth like leather. Like a leather wallet. A bulging wallet," he moaned, rubbing the piece of chocolate until it was in danger of disappearing altogether.

"Snap it next to your ear. What does it sound like?"

"Like an accomplice's stolen pickup," he murmured.

"Now, at last, eat it."

He popped the chocolate into his mouth and chewed it thoughtfully.

"It tastes like guilt," he groaned, and burst into tears.

The Tree

BY Zeta Moore, *Grade 11*

FROM *Young Writers Camp with Local Authors, Summer 2009*

THE TREE HAD BEEN FORCED onto its side by the storm the previous night. Some of its branches had cracked off. One had hit the living room window. Cracked the glass. Our cat stepped in it. Mom yelled because she thought I'd gotten the cat into it. What could I have done?

We were moving the next day, so I didn't take it to heart. I was looking out the window—at the aforementioned tree, you know—and it made me cry. My brother Adam said, "Come on," so I hurried up and followed him out to our car.

We drove behind the U-Haul to our new house, which was like two states away. That was too long in the car. We had to stop because Adam's stomach and cars aren't compatible, and I wasn't able to open up my window fast enough, so he puked on my lap. When we reached our new house, I couldn't leave the car.

"Come on, Anton," said Mom. But I couldn't. Nails forced themselves through my feet when my eyes caught the tree, fully erect, leaning on the roof.

"Anton, you okay?" My dad hadn't left the car either. He was reading the paper.

"No."

"What's up? Moving getting to you?"

I shook my head.

"What is it?"

"That tree."

"What?"

"There." I pointed, and he squinted and leaned forward. "It's at our old house."

"It looks familiar," he said. "It's not the same, but those trees are common." Hmm, Dad may not have been in his right mind.

I knew it was, though. I was glad I'd told him.

- 2 -

SCHOOL STARTED THE NEXT DAY. There weren't any kids I liked. I'll admit, I didn't throw my back out trying to meet people. I wanted them to be willing to know me, you know? Sad thing is, I knew there wasn't a lot to be curious about. I had brown hair, brown eyes. Mostly punk clothes. No surprise to anyone.

My favorite class was English. Writing was my strong suit. I especially liked writing about the strange, and frequently used words like "phosphorescent" to sound more eloquent than I was or am. Hey, look at me! I decided to write about the tree when I was supposed to be brainstorming about how I'd write my essay on agriculture. The tree's here. It was at my old house. What's wrong?

- 3 -

BUT THE TREE. The tree's my main focus. I walked up to it when I got home and leaned against its shortest branch. Heaved a sigh. It didn't move. Didn't talk.

"Dinner's ready," said Adam.

"What? Now?"

That night, something rocked against my window. Hard. I lifted my blanket over my shoulders and hoisted myself up. I slipped out of bed and walked across the room, found the tree bobbing against the window. I flicked the glass. Puckered my lips. It didn't stop. I didn't know what I was doing until Adam came and I was hitting my head against the window with an equal amount of ferocity. He held me and said, "*Anton*."

My parents came in. I talked, but kept my eyes on the tree. It remained calm.

I hated it.

IN THE LIBRARY, I went to the nature section and got out this big book of trees drawn in charcoal with gray pages that were nearly out of their binding, worn away with age and eager fingers. Ash trees. Yew trees. It was an ash tree. The picture was tattooed in my brain. I dog-eared a few pages, checked the book out.

My friends thought I was crazy. "What're you doing?" they said.

You may think these friends you're meeting are from my school. They were from my old school. They'd phone me. I'd ditch gym in the bathroom, reel them in.

"What're you gonna do with a book about trees?" Mork was, like, insane about nature, but he didn't understand why people read about it. He thought it was meant to be explored rather than dictated by another nature buff like himself. Actually, he was like that about most things, which was why his writing sucked—if you don't read, you don't write well. You knew that.

"I'm going to look up ash trees."

"Why? Don't you have an ash tree in your yard? You were telling me about one—"

"I do. I'm researching them. And that tree, yeah, the same exact one was at my old house."

"Maybe someone planted the same tree in your yard."

"No, man, they're the *same.*"

"I gotta go. Bye."

"Wait. Since they're the same, why do you think it's at my house? I've been think—"

"You need to get off LSD, man. Bye." He hung up.

Only rock stars took that.

- 5 -

I DIDN'T DO MY HOMEWORK. I ditched after-school tutoring. During all this, the tree became less important. It got weak when it learned I didn't care about it, yet the fact that I knew it was weak should've made it realize that I still was paying attention to it. It didn't. Then my dad got a call.

"We're moving again."

"What?"

I ran and crawled under our front porch and before I knew it, foreign sounds were coming out and shaking me. Out of the corner of my eye, I saw the tree. I'd read in the book about the telltale signs of a sick tree. The signs I saw told me it was dying.

- 6 -

OUR NEW HOUSE wasn't anything special. I poured over the front lawn. No tree. Went around to the back. No tree. Sides. I didn't understand. *Why aren't you here? You're not gonna leave me, are you? I love you and I don't know you.* It simply wasn't there.

It was when I was walking to school the following morning that my heart jolted. There it was, by a streetlamp.

I pulled it into my arms and it said, "Thank you." I didn't allow myself to be shocked. "Thank you."

"Why d'you keep coming?" No answer. "You're dying."

"Preserve my soul," it said.

"Why?"

"You saw my beauty. Enjoyed my company."

"I did?"

"Constance. You understand the benefits of constancy." The wind whistled through its branches. My eyes shut on their own, and a picture of the tree was etched in my mind. It slowly grew faint and eventually gave itself to the wind. And the tree left me.

Not entirely, though.

It's never goodbye.

Waiting

BY Hannah Westerberg, *Grade 6*
FROM *Poemography, Fall 2009*

The rose is perfect   63
sweet-smelling and beautiful
surrounded by metal and leaves
waiting
waiting to be chosen.
For what?
A young girl's hair, a bouquet
A he loves me, he loves me not
Anything—
For even perfection of the rose
will not mean anything unless
It is discovered.

FIELD TRIPS

Three mornings a week throughout the school year, teachers bring their students to 826CHI for a high-energy morning of great writing. 826CHI field trips take many forms: personal statements for college applications; an imagery-inspired activity that spins hilarious short stories out of magazine scraps; even food-inspired memoir writing (we've found that students have no shortage of things to say about Funyuns®). Many classes join us for Small Group Bookmaking, where students work in groups to create offbeat literary masterpieces in the span of two hours. Several of the following stories, such as "Weldi and the Cheese Incident" and "The Secret's Out," are the result of this particular trip.

The most popular field trip is Storytelling & Bookmaking, in which students are charged with a very serious task: Admiral Moody*, our chronically cranky, mysteriously unseen boss, is demanding ONE GREAT AND ORIGINAL STORY, and if he doesn't have it by the end of the morning, every single person at 826 will be fired! Working as a team, students collaborate on a story that will hopefully save the day, only to have Admiral Moody stipulate at a critical, cliffhanger moment (often via karaoke machine) that one book alone simply will not do—he's going to need more like twenty-seven stories. (Seriously. What is it with this guy?) To sort out this predicament, each student must find a resolution and finish the story his or her own way, complete with illustration, author bio, and mustachioed author photo.

Many of the stories featured in this section are the product of classroom collaborations created at the behest of Admiral Moody. We'd be grateful if you could finish them. It's allergy season, and our jobs are on the line.

---

*Curmudgeon of a publisher highly allergic to everything from dogs to doggerel and—most especially—to children. To our eternal chagrin, he is constantly grouchy because of his sinuses.

The Adventures of Takito and Mavo

BY The Students in Mrs. Jops's 2nd Grade Class
FROM *Peterson Elementary School, Spring 2009*

ONCE UPON A TIME, in the delicious city of Tongueville, there lived a talking, crunchy taco named Takito. Takito liked to walk his avocado dog, Mavo, along the beautiful beach near their house. When they got to the beach, Takito and Mavo loved to take long swims in the Salad Ocean, and this ocean was no ordinary body of water: it was filled with celery, tomatoes, meat, some spinach, tofu, and little onion rings.

Unfortunately, Mavo was a bit of a naughty dog. Whenever Takito would take him to the beach, Mavo would always try to eat things out of the ocean. In fact, he would eat anything and everything he saw, whether it was garbage, small rocks, dirt—and sometimes, things that were in Takito's pockets!

One day, Mavo was especially hungry, and he began to chase Takito around the beach, trying to take a bite out of him.

"Mavo!" scolded Takito. "Stop this nonsense right now!"

"But you look so delicious," Mavo replied, "and I'm really hungry!"

Takito had an idea. He would try to get Mavo something more healthy to eat. Something that was not Takito. To do this, they would have to go the sushi store all the way at the bottom of the Salad Ocean.

Takito and Mavo went to the shore and climbed into their submarine-sandwich-shaped submarine and began to descend to the ocean floor. The ride was going smoothly until they felt a big BUMP.

"What in Tongueville was *that*?" asked Takito.

No sooner had Takito asked the question than they felt another BUMP. It was a tomato torpedo!

Mavo barked, "Someone is attacking us!"

"Oh no!" cried Takito. "It must be the Tomato Man!"

WILL TAKITO AND MAVO ESCAPE IN TIME FOR DINNER? WHAT KIND OF SUSHI LURKS BENEATH THE DEPTHS OF A SALAD OCEAN? IS TOMATO MAN TECHNICALLY A FRUIT? HELP OUR FRIENDS SOLVE THIS DIETARY DILEMMA AND FINISH THE STORY!

The Diamond Wars

BY The Students in Mr. Zielinski's 4th–6th Grade Class
FROM *Drummond Montessori School, Fall 2009*

IN A FLAMING VOLCANO set deep in the hills of Kentucky, the famous Kedon Diamond was floating in a bubble of lava. Four brothers, Carnermanooga, Jaminono, Penguin, and Akuna, were searching for the diamond, trying to prevent the Lava Monsters from getting it first.

The Lava Monsters desired the diamond because it would allow them to leave the volcano and terrorize people all over the world. The four brothers would do anything to stop them. These weren't just any brothers, though—they were Chalk Warriors! Their superpower was to draw people, who would come to life as break-dance fighters.

"Let's make a plan!" shouted Akuna.

"I agree," Penguin said. "Let's try to distract them by surrounding them with break-dance fighters!"

"All right, let's do it!" yelled Jaminono.

The brothers surveyed the territory and found a ridge to stand on.

"Let's get into position," Carnermanooga announced heroically.

The brothers assembled into a rhombus. Using their chalk swords, they drew an army of goblin break-dance fighters. The break-dance fighters popped out, making a loud *BOOM*! The chalk drawings created twenty-five break-dance fighters every second.

Suddenly, Carnermanooga threw his hands in the air. In a frantic voice, he shouted, "Wait, I just heard on the radio that there's a 25% discount on everything at Target, and I think the Lava Monsters are invading it by shopping! There's lava everywhere and no one else can buy anything!"

"Panic!" yelled Akuna.

The brothers and their break-dancing goblins ran into the heart of the volcano, at the bottom of which there happened to be a Target retail store.

"Are you *kidding* me?!" bellowed Penguin.

The brothers stood before a gigantic, three-floor Target filled with awesome toys and video games, things that people actually wanted. Unknown to the brothers, the Kedon Diamond was hidden beneath the secret fourth floor of the shopping facility.

While the brothers were distracted by all of the incredible discounts, the Lava Monsters snuck up on them. One of them picked up a bicycle and threw it at Jaminono.

As the bicycle soared through the air, Jaminono exclaimed, "That bicycle is practically jumping at me! I wonder how much it is?"

The bicycle conked Jaminono in the head, sending him falling down a bunch of stairs. When he landed on the hidden fourth floor, he broke through the floorboards. There, Jaminono saw the diamond.

Just then, two Lava Monsters came after Jaminono. Thinking fast, he broke his chalk in two and hurled the pieces at his attackers. When the chalk touched the Lava Monsters, they exploded! Jaminono took a piece of chalk and thrust it into the diamond, and the Lava Monsters disappeared forever.

That is how the brothers saved the world.

Except Carnermanooga, who was still shopping.

73

The Nutty Adventures of Tutu Nutty-Nuts

BY The Students in Ms. Venegas's 2nd Grade Class
FROM *LaSalle Language Academy, Spring 2009*

ONCE UPON A TIME, in the very exciting, exotic, Mesozoic era of Finoodeland, there lived a talking prehistoric flying squirrel named Tutu Nutty-Nuts. Tutu Nutty-Nuts was brown with red polka dots and yellow feet. He also had a 300-foot-long tail.

Tutu was an old-fashioned cowboy. He chased cows all along the noodley plains of the treetop village of Finoodeland. It was a truly exhausting job, and he had to drink one billion gallons of coconut coffee each day just to keep up with those wily flying cows.

One summer, there was a horrendous drought in Finoodeland. Among the many problems this caused, there was not enough rain to water the coconuts that Tutu and all of the prehistoric flying squirrels used to make their coffee. Tutu decided to go and search for more sources of coconut coffee so that he and all the other flying squirrels could stay awake and do their jobs. He also decided to take his favorite cow of the herd, Babushka.

The first place that Tutu and Babushka traveled to was Boston. But as they arrived, they saw that not only was it a very urban area without much farming, there were also a bunch of people throwing tea into the ocean.

"Isn't that weird?" Tutu said to Babushka.

"That is really weird," Babushka said. "I think we should go someplace else."

The very next place they flew was the magical island of Ganalda. But the weather on Ganalda was very, very odd: one day it would be sunny, the next it would rain, all year round. This made it nearly impossible to grow the right kinds of nuts and fruits that the prehistoric flying squirrels used to make coffee.

"Oh, no!" said Tutu. "What are we going to do?"

Will Tutu and Babushka regulate the Ganaldian weather? Can Babushka convince her wily friends to behave? Will the old-fashioned cowboys switch to herbal tea? Help our hero stay alert by finishing the story!

The Secret's Out

BY The Students in Ms. Hammer's 5th Grade Class
FROM *San Miguel School, Spring 2009*

ONCE UPON A TIME in Hollywood there lived two lovely friends named Donea and Keyshia Cole. Donea, a cheetah, was born in a cave. She always wore a beautiful pink dress with sparkling diamonds all over. Donea, who walked on two legs, also loved to wear a pair of high-heeled purple boots and a shining golden crown. She liked to eat fried chicken, macaroni, and dinosaurs.

Donea's best friend was Keyshia Cole. Keyshia Cole was a breath-taking lionness who loved chicken noodle soup with a soda on the side. Most days, she wore a purple dress with flower designs on the side.

Every Saturday night at nine o'clock, Donea and Keyshia Cole would go to the park to sing "I Like the Way You Move" for a huge audience. The crowd loved them. They were pop stars! Life was good, and they were very happy together.

That is, until one day, when trouble (and love) struck.

Donea and Keyshia Cole were walking to the park on a rainy day—because they had heard there was going to be a wild Halloween party for all of Hollywood—when they first laid eyes on Hip-Hop Harry, the new kid in town. Hip-Hop Harry was the hairiest hitch-up in the entire world. Even his eyes and mouth were hairy, and his arms were even hairier. He was wearing a jersey (Number 1), because he played basketball with the Chicago Bulls. He had arrived at 6:00PM to register at his swanky hotel, and then gone straight to the party.

As soon as Donea and Keyshia Cole saw Hip-Hop Harry they both screamed at the exact same time, "I got dibs on that man!"

Then they turned to each other and angrily snapped, "What type of friend are you?"

Upset, the two lovely ladies and former friends walked away from each other.

Later that night, after the party, Donea looked out her window and saw Hip-Hop Harry walking by her house. She had an idea.

Donea pretended to be sick and said out the window, "Cough, cough, I am very sick. Can you help me?"

Hip-Hop Harry ran to the window and said, "What can I bring you?"

The two started talking and were having a good time, when suddenly Keyshia Cole saw them laughing with each other and stormed over.

"What are you doing with Hip-Hop Harry, Donea? He doesn't like you!"

Hip-Hop Harry looked confused.

He said, "I like both of you, but I already have my little Secret." With that, he walked away and went back to his hairy, hairy hotel room.

Keyshia Cole and Donea were very angry. They didn't understand what he had been talking about with his secret. They started arguing about Hip-Hop Harry, and Donea slammed her window, shouting, "Never talk to me again!"

The next morning, the two ladies both decided they were going to try to win over their crush. They followed him out of his hotel, all the way to the park. Suddenly, they looked up and saw Hip-Hop Harry running towards another lady: a giant hippo (who was a little bit hairy, just like him).

Keyshia Cole and Donea ran up to Hip-Hop Harry and asked, "Who is that? Why are you with this big, hairy hippo?"

Hip-Hop Harry turned to them and made introductions: "Donea, Keyshia Cole, this is my fiancée, Secret."

Keyshia Cole and Donea faced each other and exclaimed, "Ooooooooooh!! That's your Secret. Now we understand."

Donea and Keyshia Cole realized they had been silly to fight over a crush, especially one who was about to be married!

The two lovely lady cats said to each other, "I'm sorry, let's be friends again." Then they realized it was almost nine o'clock. So the four animals all walked back to the audience waiting at the park and sang "Why Can't We Be Friends" together. From that day forward, they were all best friends 'til the end.

Enchanting Superfish's Mission

BY The Students in Mrs. Kendt's 2nd Grade Class
FROM *South Loop Elementary School, Spring 2009*

ONE MORNING, SUPERFISH woke up in his super-secret house in his fishbowl. He was in the basement of a house in Hawaii. As usual, Superfish swam out of bed and went to his secret lab to put on his supersuit; it was made out of leather. Superfish then sat down and ate his superfishfood breakfast, which consisted of pencils, ink, and alien sauce.

Just then, Superfish got an urgent message from his boss, Bob the penguin. Bob, who lived in Egypt, used his mind powers to talk to Superfish.

"Superfish! There is a robbery in New York City! Please go rescue the people!" yelled Bob the Penguin.

"I'm on it!" replied Superfish. He twisted his eyeball and turned off his mental voice receiver.

Superfish woke up Josh the Junior Superfish, who slept on the living room couch. They hopped out of the fishbowl, stood on the windowsill, and jumped with might! They got to New York in five seconds.

"Superfish, look at your watch so we can see where the robbery is," said Josh.

"Oh, yes, now I remember!" said Superfish, as he put his superfin to his superforehead. Superfish looked at his watch, and it told him where to go to rescue the people. Superfish pressed two buttons on the watch, and his superfish car showed up. He and Josh hopped in, and the car flew superspeed above the traffic.

Superfish and Josh arrived at the scene of the crime, and it was a bank! The wall of the bank was broken, and it had fallen forward in one piece.

WHO IS ROBBING THE BIG APPLE BANK? CAN SUPERFISH FOIL THEIR DASTARDLY PLANS? WILL JOSH EVER GET HIS OWN APARTMENT? IT'S UP TO YOU TO WRITE A SUPER ENDING AND HELP US FINISH THE STORY!

Weldi and the Cheese Incident

BY The Students in Mrs. Nelson's 7th Grade Class
FROM *Belding School, Winter 2009*

THERE ONCE WAS a colony of talking marshmallows that lived on planet Googala, a tiny planet that existed inside Mars. Everyone in the colony was extremely fond of canned cheese, a very fattening food that was shipped to Googala from Venus. This was all the marshmallows ate.

In the entire colony of talking marshmallows, there was one unique marshmallow named Weldi. Weldi hated canned cheese. He only liked gourmet cheese and pickles, which he made himself, in his bedroom. Since he was a little mallow, all of the other canned cheese-loving marshmallows would make fun of him and pile canned cheese all over him every chance they got.

Weldi's parents were very displeased by the behavior of their son's peers. They tried talking to the principal of the school, Ms. Mallowbottom, but the principal just brushed them off. "It's your son's problem, not mine! Canned cheese is a wonderful delicacy on our planet. If he doesn't like it, then the other students have every right to make fun of him."

The parents, with frustrated expressions on their marshmallow faces, sulked and stomped out of the school. They felt they had no choice—on the ride home in their watermelon car, the two concerned mallows decided that they would see if they could get Weldi to like canned cheese.

For the next three days, Weldi's parents kept their son home from school and pleaded with him from morning until night to give up his gourmet cheese and homemade pickles for the much more socially acceptable canned cheese. Weldi wouldn't budge. Instead, he stayed in bed all day because he was so sad.

83

Eventually, Weldi got sick of lying in bed and started thinking about what he could do to change the minds of his fellow Googalians with regard to gourmet cheese and pickles.

"Maybe," he thought to himself, "I can call my friend Steve who works at the canned cheese shipping and receiving yard..." A giant light bulb suddenly popped up over his head.

"Dang, that light bulb is hot," he said, as he picked up his cell phone and dialed up Steve. "Hey buddy, I need a favor."

The next day, everyone in the town was anxiously waiting for the new shipment of canned cheese. As the succession of delivery ships pulled in, everyone rushed to them. The doors opened slowly, slowly, slowly...

"WHAT!" screamed an anonymous marshmallow in the crowd. Soon everyone was going crazy.

"That's not canned cheese!"

The ships were full of gourmet cheese and pickles.

Weldi watched from his bedroom window as his scheme unfolded and contemplated his next move. He went downstairs, hopped on his bike, and zoomed into the rioting crowd. He climbed on top of one of the delivery ships and pulled out a giant megaphone.

"Attention marshmallows!" Weldi hollered. "I realize this is not the shipment of canned cheese you've been waiting for. Instead, I've arranged for that shipment to go to Pluto, and for Googala to receive mass amounts of gourmet cheese and pickles."

Everyone screamed.

"Wait! Wait!" Weldi continued. "Hear me out!"

As Weldi explained how hurt he had been by all the other marshmallows his whole life, the crowd began pushing the ships around in fury.

"WE WANT OUR CANNED CHEESE!" they screamed in unison.

At one point, the riotous jostling caused a piece of gourmet cheese to fall from a ship's deck into the mouth of a crowd member. The marshmallow swallowed the cheese and a wave of enjoyment washed over him. He became mellow and quite content, and sat down to relax with more gourmet cheese away from the crowd. Eventually a few more of the angry marshmallows tasted the gourmet cheese and pickles—and everyone loved them. Before long, the planet was quiet because everyone was eating Weldi's favorite foods.

"We're so sorry, Weldi," his classmates said, their mouths full of gourmet cheese. "We shouldn't have been so quick to insult you just because you were different."

With that, the crowd formed a group hug around Weldi. From that day forward, everything was happy—and much more gourmet—on planet Googala.

Back2Back Planet and the Many Big Problems

BY The Students in Mrs. Peña's 3rd Grade Class

FROM *Inter-American Magnet School, Winter 2009*

ON BACK2BACK PLANET there were two lands that did not care for one another. On one side of the great Orange Juice Lake lived the people of Goonieland. The inhabitants were made of green, blue, and red Jell-O. The Goonies were a very friendly people who liked to build houses out of lollipops and hot Cheetos. On the other side of the lake lived the Lego-people of Legoland. They, of course, were made of Legos, but they were not friendly like the Goonies. Instead of building houses, the Legopeople were lazy. They slept all day and played mean pranks on the Goonies, like stealing their banana boats. *AND* they would never say, "Sorry."

The ruler of Goonieland was named Mayor Hoonie Goonie. He was fat and made of red Jell-O with Jolly Ranchers for a crown. All the Goonies in Goonieland loved the

Mayor. Across the lake, it was a different story. They were ruled by Scary Popsicle, an evil king.

One day, King Scary Popsicle came up with a very mean and scary plan. He told all the people of Legoland to go across the Orange Juice Lake and knock down the Goonies' lollipop-and-Cheeto houses.

At exactly midnight, when all the Goonies were asleep on their chocolate beds with pickle pillows and cotton candy sheets, the Legopeople came ashore. To keep the Goonie people asleep, the Legopeople played their favorite relaxing music, "Rock-a-Bye-Candy."

The Legopeople knocked down every single house in Goonieland, and Scary Popsicle even stole the Jolly Rancher crown from Mayor Hoonie Goonie!

The next day, when Mayor Hoonie Goonie woke up, he yelled, "Egg Salad! Where's my crown?!" Then, when he walked outside, he saw that all the lollipop houses had been torn down.

One of the Goonies ran up to the Mayor and said, "We need to strike back against the evil King Scary Popsicle! What are we going to do?"

CAN THE GOONIES DEFEAT KING SCARY POPSICLE? WILL MAYOR HOONIE GOONIE RECOVER HIS CROWN? IS "ROCK-A-BYE-CANDY" AVAILABLE ON VINYL? WITH YOUR HELP, WE CAN BRING THE GOONIES AND THE LEGOPEOPLE TOGETHER AND FINISH THE STORY!

The Bleach Problem

BY The Students in Ms. Parise's 5th Grade Class
FROM *Walsh Elementary School, Winter 2010*

[Editors' note: Don't drink bleach.]

ONCE UPON A TIME, there was a vampire named Blaze who loved bleach. He drank it daily to keep his ghoulishly pale color.

One morning, as Blaze sat in his small dungeon, in his favorite multicolored shirt and pink boxers, he combed his shoulder-length hair and realized he was thirsty. But there was a problem: it was daylight, and he couldn't go outside to get bleach.

He stroked his thin mustache. "Oh, whatever, I'll wait a little longer. Besides, *Charlie Brown* is on."

But then, a *Tom and Jerry* marathon came on television, and Blaze couldn't be pulled away from his favorite show. He fell asleep and woke the next day so thirsty he couldn't get out of his coffin. Blaze reached for his phone with all of his might to call his friend Eddie. The phone rang and rang and rang, but Eddie did not answer.

"Oh my God. Oh my God. Oh, oh my God," Blaze rasped. "Eddie, answer, *please*. I need you."

Suddenly, Blaze's phone rang. He reached for his phone, but fell out of the coffin. Good thing he had his phone on the floor. He heard Eddie's voice, "Hello?"

"Eddie? I need bleach really, really badly. I'm so thirsty, and if I don't get any bleach, I will suffer and disappear," Blaze wheezed.

"I better go to the store to buy bleach," Eddie said quickly before he hung up.

Eddie ran out of his house and sprinted the five blocks to the grocery store. He walked to the register, but as he stood waiting in line he imagined Blaze disappearing little by little without bleach. Panicking, he ran for the door. Two security guards, wearing nametags that read TOM and DOUG, stepped in front of him.

"Hey, where do you think you're going with that bleach?" they demanded.

"I need to get this bleach to my friend. If he doesn't drink the bleach he will disappear forever," Eddie said.

Tom and Doug gave each other a funny look before starting to laugh.

"You're not getting away with this," Tom said. The security guards grabbed Eddie and the bleach.

"Hey, Tom, Doug, let him go," Eddie heard a voice behind him say. He turned around to see a woman wearing a nametag that said Crystal—Store Manager standing behind him.

"I'll pay you back," Eddie promised, before he sprinted the five blocks to Blaze's.

When Eddie got to the dungeon, Blaze's feet and hands had already disappeared, so Eddie had to pour the bleach into Blaze's mouth. Almost instantly, Eddie could see Blaze's feet and hands start to come back. He was going to be okay.

"Thanks, Eddie," said Blaze. "If you ever need anything from me, call me and I'll be there. Forever."

With his restored hands, Blaze grabbed the remote and turned on the television. *Charlie Brown* was on.

Crayon and Johnny's Adventures

BY The Students in Mrs. LeBlanc's 4th Grade Class
FROM *The Chicago Academy, Fall 2009*

CRAYON THE CRAYFISH was great friends with Johnny the Lobster. Crayon drew pictures for an art gallery owned by Johnny. He specialized in painting scenes of sharks eating pasta.

Before long, a school of sharks gathered outside the gallery and began protesting the paintings. They were all very angry, because sharks don't eat pasta.

Inside the gallery, Johnny and Crayon were getting nervous and plotting their next move.

Big Shark, the shark leader, shouted in to them, "What if we drew pictures of you eating *crayons?*"

The sharks decided to climb through a window to get into the gallery to try to talk to Johnny and Crayon. But that wasn't all—the sharks decided to take the paintings when

Johnny and Crayon weren't looking and replace them with their own.

When Crayon wasn't looking, Big Shark drew a picture of a shark on Crayon's back. Johnny noticed the picture and told Crayon, "There's a shark on your back!"

"Get it off me! Get it off!" yelled Crayon.

Johnny examined the drawing on his friend's back and surveyed the room.

"It's a painting," he exclaimed, "but there are the *real* sharks! And our paintings have been replaced!"

They looked around and saw that all the paintings were of Crayon and Johnny eating crayons. In the corner of each painting was scrawled "SHARKS RULE!"

92

WILL CRAYON AND JOHNNY ESCAPE THE SHARKS? CAN THE TWO FRIENDS SALVAGE THEIR ARTWORK? CAN THE SHARKS BE CONVINCED TO ENJOY MOSTACCIOLI? HELP OUR CHARACTERS RESOLVE THEIR ARTISTIC DIFFERENCES AND FINISH THE STORY!

Perry the Robot Mouse and his Exclusive Adventure Watch

BY The Students in Miss Militello's 5th Grade Class
FROM *Chase Elementary School, Winter 2009*

ONCE THERE WAS A MULTICOLORED, time-traveling robot mouse named Perry. Perry had x-ray vision, could transform at will, and lived on his own private moon. He also had a special watch that allowed him to travel into the future (and the past, if he wished).

One day, while rock climbing, Perry fell and cracked his watch! Suddenly, he was transported to the year 7278. He was surprised to see that in the year 7278, the world had flooded, so everyone lived in holographic floating houses.

"Holy Robot Moly!" Perry exclaimed.

Perry knew he had to find special silver tools to fix his watch so that he could go home. He used his x-ray vision to search for the tools. Unfortunately, once he located the tools, he saw that they were guarded by a horde of giant mechanical electric sharks.

Thinking quickly, Perry transformed into a camouflaged submarine and sped through the water. He stealthily puttered by the sharks, but one especially large shark perked up his nose.

"I smell a mouse!" shouted the shark. He turned and began to swim after Perry. "He's after the special tools!"

The shark gulped down the treasure chest that held the special tools, and then opened his gigantic, sparking mouth and swallowed Perry whole! Perry landed in the electric shark's stomach, inside of which was a humming engine. Perry scurried around the shark's belly and found the key to the treasure chest hidden in the heart.

Meanwhile, the shark was beginning to feel guilty.

"Oh dear!" thought the shark. "Maybe we could have been friends."

Perry tickled the shark inside his mechanical belly, and the shark began to laugh. When he opened his huge mouth to let out a chuckle, Perry raced from his stomach into a floating house.

"Thank you!" Perry called out to the confused shark.

Using the tools, Perry quickly fixed his watch and traveled back to his home on the moon in the year 2010. He held a welcome home party with his robot mice friends, and told them about his adventures. Perry also made a friendly electric shark and sent it to the year of 7278 as a thank-you gift. He included a time-traveling watch so that the shark and his new friend could come back in time and visit.

Panda-Pig Bob Meets the Scary Bear-agon!

BY The Students in Mrs. Zanin's 3rd Grade Class
FROM *Mark Sheridan Academy, Fall 2009*

BOB THE PANDA-PIG lived in a cave in the woods behind a Burger King. He usually wore a black and white skirt and a shirt with purple flames. One of Bob's favorite things was to tell jokes to his space bunny friend, Salami.

"What is a ghost's favorite ride at a carnival?" asked Bob.

"I don't know," said Salami.

"A *roller ghoster!*" squealed Bob.

Salami the space bunny laughed so hard he thought his brain was about to explode. Suddenly, the clouds got dark. Bob and Salami heard a roar of thunder and they saw fire shooting from the back of the cave.

"What is *that*?!" cried Bob.

"Uh oh!" said Salami. "I laughed so hard I woke up some scary creature."

Out of the darkness rose the scariest creature in the whole world. It had three heads—one was a bear and two were dragons. One half of the creature's body was black fur and the other was covered in red scales.

"Oh NO!" yelled Salami. "It's a bear-agon! Run!"

Bob and Salami ran as fast as they could out of the cave and into the Burger King where they hid in the kitchen. Just then, the bear-agon smelled the food in the kitchen and began heading toward it.

"I'm so hungry," growled the bear-agon, "I've been hibernating for 2,000 years!"

WILL BOB AND SALAMI ESCAPE THE BEAR-AGON? WHAT KIND OF SNACK WILL SATISFY A GROGGY MONSTER? WILL BOB EVER LEARN NEW JOKES? HAVE IT YOUR WAY AND FINISH THE STORY!

IN-SCHOOLS

Throughout the school year, 826CHI staff and volunteers head into Chicago Public Schools to work on projects at a teacher's request. Work through the in-schools program may be short- or long-term, sending tutors into the classroom regularly for a month, a semester, or even a year. In addition to classroom teacher-directed projects, 826CHI has also designed activities that complement classroom activities and address curricular needs.

Each day is a new adventure: we may be helping students polish up a Young Authors book; working on a journalism project; celebrating Poetry Month; putting together a literary magazine; or helping revise the final draft of an expository essay. This section features just a few of the pieces created as part of these projects.

Ms. Dunn Should Get a Mohawk: A Persuasive Essay

BY Joel Flores, Mariah Gonzalez, Cindy Salgado, Diego Villegas, and Marques Ward-Gill, *Grade 6*
FROM *Andersen School, Winter 2010*

WE BELIEVE THAT OUR TEACHER, Ms. Dunn, should get a Mohawk for three primary reasons that we shall go over in this essay. It would be a great idea that would be hilarious, unique, and multicolored.

Ms. Dunn, the first reason we think that you should get a Mohawk is that your hair grows quickly, and you have your whole life to have your hair different lengths. You may say, "But I don't want to cut off all my hair." We would like to say in response to that, "Even if you do not like the style and length, your hair will grow back, and you might even get used to it." We think that the Mohawk should be long, sharp, and split in half at the top like sliced meat—and Xtreme-gelled out for shade in the summer.

Secondly, we believe that more people will look up to you if you get a Mohawk. Other teachers may even get jealous and try the same style. Just think, Ms. Dunn—you could be an inspiration to everyone around you! You may argue, "But it's important for me to look professional at my job." In response to this, we guarantee that people will admire you and feel awed by your sense of style. We also think that you would be famous, and maybe the first person working in Chicago Public Schools to have a Mohawk!

Third, and finally, Ms. Dunn, we think that you should have a Mohawk because people will love seeing you stand out, as well as seeing you put yourself out there to show the true you. We think that you will see this happen if you decide to have a rainbow-colored Mohawk. Also, you would look like a shark while swimming, but you would not get harpooned because of the rainbow colors. Your Mohawk wouldn't be ruined, because you would have to keep your head above the water, due to the Xtreme gel holding up your Mohawk. You may argue, "But it's too distracting. No one will pay attention to me if I get a Mohawk." We promise you that people will be dazzled and they will easily spot you and pay attention to you. It will inspire us as students to see that not all people have everything in common, and how being different shows who you really are.

In conclusion, Ms. Dunn, there are three great reasons why you should be an amazing "Rock Star" and get a Mohawk. We hope that you will consider our suggestion seriously and think about rockin' a Mohawk. We thank you for your time and consideration.

The Chicago Bears Are Secretly Aliens: A Persuasive Essay

BY Daniel Gonzalez and Tatiana Jackson, *Grade 8*
FROM *Andersen School, Winter 2010*

EVEN THOUGH YOU do not know it, we are being invaded by aliens: the Chicago Bears are secretly aliens disguised as football players. Our reasoning for this is supported by the fact that the Bears can withstand cold weather, the shape of Soldier Field is perfect for aliens, and because of how badly the Bears played this season.

The first reason why it is obvious that the Bears are aliens is that they can withstand absolutely freezing weather. It is known that aliens' ice cold, blue scales indicate they live in a colder part of the galaxy. When it's approximately –34°C, they are out there playing like it is 74°F outside. On top of that, they are usually drinking ice cold Gatorade, which is proven among Andersen School students to give you a headache in sub-zero temperatures.

Another reason behind our argument is the shape of Soldier Field. Its large, oval shape is set very deep underground so that the shape-shifting aliens can land their ship before games. (As a side note, while they were playing in December, a fan threw pop at the field and it was dripping from midair. They forfeited the game, possibly to prevent their technologically advanced uniforms from exploding, causing a battle with the human fans.)

The final reason proving this theory is that the Bears played horribly this season, winning only 7 games and losing 9. The Bears' quarterback, Jay Cutler, didn't know what to do when he saw the football. Or, as news reporter Ryan Seacrest said, "It was like he had never seen or heard of football in his entire life."

So, you tell us—aliens or not? Remember: withstanding freezing cold weather, the shape of Soldier Field, and their vile season.

Our School Mascot Should Be a Unicorn: A Persuasive Essay

BY Aurea Ascencio, Eduardo Diaz, and Zulema Hernandez,
Grade 8
FROM *Andersen School, Winter 2010*

WE BELIEVE OUR SCHOOL mascot should be a unicorn for several reasons. First, it brings out the uniqueness of our school. Second, our school was named after a man named Hans Christian Andersen, who wrote fairy tales. Third, the unicorn is something beautiful and outstanding that catches peoples' attention.

The first reason our school's mascot should be a unicorn is because this unique mascot brings out the mesmerizing coolness of Andersen School. Currently, our mascot is an eagle. Eagles are everywhere. They are used by lots of schools as mascots, and you can find them on clothes, notebooks, and lots of other things. Everybody at Andersen has a good imagination and everybody here is different. Really, a unicorn represents how we are different much better than an eagle.

Some people may not want to make the unicorn our mascot because they may worry that it will cost a lot of money to change everything, like the images and colors in the school. We *are* in a recession. However, we can always make our own mascot gear and buy our own supplies and others could help out. We could hold a student-led fund-raiser to redo the mascot throughout the school. Alternatively, we could catch a live unicorn to use for the school and we could also charge people for rides as a way to raise more money for the necessary changes. We haven't caught one at the time of this essay, but we're pretty sure we could find one in Hawaii.

The second reason we have is that, well, the school was named after Hans Christian Andersen. He lived in Denmark in the 1800's and wrote stories such as "The Little Mermaid." It would be nice to have a mascot that stands for the many fairy tales that he wrote, and unicorns are very mythical. Some people may not believe in unicorns, but we believe this isn't really the point. The unicorn is a nice animal that just stands out, and it's a great way to create more school spirit. The unicorn allows kids to use their imaginations—just like Hans Christian Andersen—and to be inspired to create and to learn.

As our final reason, we think that the unicorn is something beautiful and it really brings people happiness. Students don't need sorrow in their lives. A beautiful thing will help them and lessen their problems by bringing them joy. People may wonder: "Can a mascot really do this?" The answer is "Yes!" With a unicorn as a mascot, we will constantly be reminded of its beauty because it will be all over the school, brightening students' days and making them happy whenever they see it on clothes, notebook covers, and painted by the front door. It's not so much about what a mascot *does* as what it means to different people. The unicorn might mean something different to each person and inspire each student in a new way.

In conclusion, a unicorn would make a very awesome mascot. The reasons we have stated—representing our uniqueness, connecting to the school's namesake, and creating greater student happiness—are just a few points to this outstanding idea. In the words of what we hope will soon be our new mascot cheer: *"GO, UNI, GO!"*

Transformed by Music:
A Profile Piece

BY Diamond Stevenson, *Grade 11*
FROM *Roberto Clemente High School, Fall 2009*

"It's like the beat drops, and I transform. I start to feel like Superman."

These are the words of Steven Garner, 23. Steven was born December 14, in Chicago, Illinois. He grew up on the west side, near Washington and Central.

His childhood was rough. Steven lived in a two-bedroom apartment with his mother, Karliee, and her boyfriend. His mom was a high school dropout, and her boyfriend was an older man who was physically and emotionally abusive. Steven attended St. Angeles, a Catholic elementary school near Central and Laramie. He barely graduated from the eighth grade. He wasn't a perfect student, but he says he was "determined to make it big in this messed up world." He attended Foreman High School. Although he admits he was rarely there, when he was, he did his best: "I can recall times when I came to school and was so angry and depressed from my home life that I distracted myself as much as possible with my schoolwork." Steven used his education as a temporary escape from his chaotic home.

During Steven's sophomore year, things got even worse. His mother's boyfriend packed up and left him and his mother to fend for themselves. Since his mother had Steven at a young age, she had dropped out of school and didn't have great job experience or opportunities. It was up to him to be the man of the house and support them. He did everything from working in restaurants to working in the streets.

For a while, it all seemed to be working out for Steven, but then he got arrested.

"Making the call to say 'Mama, I got locked up,' was so hard for me, I cried," he remembers. Immediately after his mom received the call, she arrived with enough money to bail him out. This experience woke him up and made him realize that working hard and legally is the best way to do things.

Steven and his mother finally saved up enough money to move themselves into a better, safer neighborhood. Steven remembers feeling happy for the first time in years. His happiness soon faded, however, when his mother began dating a new boyfriend, Greg. Steven hated Greg and he never hid it. Every day they argued. They couldn't stand to be in the same room with each other.

Then, after eight months of arguing every day, Greg introduced Steven to something that changed his life: Music.

Greg was a producer. He made beats for his friends to sing to, rap to, and to sell. Steven was intrigued by the world of music, and after his first day in the studio he knew he was addicted to the art of songwriting and music production. Before long, the rivalry between Steven and Greg ceased, and their mutual love for music provided the building blocks of their relationship.

Steven's first experience was writing a verse on a track with his cousin. He got the beat and started writing. He recalls it felt as though "the music magically came out the tip of the pen. It felt so natural. That day, I fell in love for the first time, and it was with music."

112

The next day, Steven woke up and found that Greg had stayed up all night putting together some studio space for them: a booth, a mic, a sound board, a keyboard, and a lot of pens and paper.

Steven began to spend numerous hours in the studio, writing and recording nonstop. Steven was now eighteen and approaching an age where he was ready to be on his own. He planned to get himself a studio apartment filled with music equipment and start his career as an artist. His new name was Stevie G.

But he changed his mind. Steven's dreams were put on hold when he decided to enlist in the army. Now, Steven says he regrets his decision: "Everything happened so fast: I was in training, and then the next thing I know I was a soldier."

Steven was somewhat traumatized by his experiences. Before his discharge, he went AWOL. Steven was getting upset during this part of our conversation and wouldn't tell me more.

When he returned from the army, Steven was a changed man. He had new views and beliefs and outlooks on life, but he still had the same dreams in mind. He returned to his mother's house and resumed making music. He got an agent and now dedicates all his time to his music.

Currently, Steven is still making songs. He is working on his second album and is determined to make it big. He says that he has been struggling all his life, and he's ready to receive the reward for his hard work.

The Perfect High School

BY Auston Ortiz, *Grade 8*
FROM *Andersen School, Winter 2010*

[In January, 826CHI visited Ms. Dunn's eighth grade classes to work with students on letters and essays about their education. They had no shortage of things to say. Many students wrote heartfelt thank you letters to former teachers, while others spent time designing their version of 'The Perfect High School'. Auston—known for his outspoken humor in class—took a slightly different take on the latter prompt, which resulted in the essay below.]

WHAT WOULD MAKE a high school perfect? Pssh, don't get me started. My current school starts too early for me. I barely want to wake up in the mornings. Instead of forcing my body to wake up, I would like to sleep in until my body is ready to wake up... or when I have to use the bathroom. I would love to start school at 2:30PM and end around six or six thirty because that's when *The Simpsons* and *Family Guy* come on.

With Ms. Novak as the head math teacher, I would look forward to math. She is like a math magician. And she would probably love to teach on a cruise ship and I would love to learn on one. Just throwing it out there. Also, it would be good for students to have some mechanical classes just in case our cars break down in the future.

Another suggestion for the perfect school would be more gym. And when I say more gym, I don't mean an extra ten minutes in the period. I mean more *classes*, like boxing. I would like to learn how to box. Hot girls would also make a high school much better. Not only hot girls, smart hot girls. That way, I could look at them and learn some stuff while I'm doing that.

If we had hot wings and fries with cheese, school would be my favorite place in the world. Wings that are on fire would be the best. Not only because they are hot wings, but also because they are delicious. Curly fries are good also, but dip them in cheese, and they are irresistible.

You've asked me what would make a high school perfect and I could keep going but I'd rather not. As long as the high school has the features that I was just listing, I would be A-okay. And, of course, if Megan Fox were our model for art class I'd be delighted, but let's not push it.

Spontaneous: A Memoir

BY Clanisha "Cocoa" White, *Grade 9*
FROM *Chicago Talent Development High School, Fall 2009*

MY NAME IS COCOA and I was scared. Constant aches and pains, constantly popping Advil. What's wrong with me? Where's my monthly Mother Nature's package? Why are my feet swelling? Am I getting big or are my clothes shrinking?

Yeah, I watch TLC and the Health Channel, and I also read pamphlets. The ones with healthy babies with big, two-teeth smiles. This can't happen. I'm definitely too young! Living inside of an illusion, afraid to tell my mom. I'm now a statistic and I am going to get stereotyped, labeled a dropout or just another girl who doesn't know who the father is. No income. Not even an eighth grade diploma yet. Just me and a big belly, and let's not forget a secret that I DO NOT

WANT TO TELL. I personally believe my family is judgmental, so I hide the fact.

I'm hungry—I've got the money and I want the special, but it won't stay down. I am tired. I want to go to the library, but there's no energy to walk, let alone talk. I'm not the typical, fast-paced Cocoa right now. Seven months in hiding, okay? When will the creation or the thing inside of me separate itself from me?

I try to drift off to my chillax spot, blanking out reality. What about the stuff Grandma used to say about taking a bath if you're in pain, or if you have a headache, take an aspirin, or what about if you are hungry, then *eat*?!

I was at school one day, feeling a little off, and I kept telling myself the feeling would go away, it's only the twenty-four hour stomach flu, or it's my menstruation finally coming on. Those were my thoughts. At the clinic, it was totally different.

At the clinic with my mom, I get to the front desk and a young office assistant gives me a little slip. You know the feeling—the little slip should have had CONFIDENTIAL on it because I don't want anyone knowing my business, not even my mom. When you get the slip you should sit as far away as possible from your mom because they ask you: *When was your last period? Are you sexually active? Do you smoke?* Or some questions I didn't know like: *What is your social security number? Do you want a vaginal birth or a cesarean section?*

When I finish, all I do is wait. I'm inside of a brightly-colored waiting room. There are a thousand and one posters that have a photo of a woman with a huge belly and her options, written in big, bold letters: ABORTION vs. ADOPTION and a friendly toll-free number that you can call to make that decision. Well, personally, I don't believe in that at all. I don't believe any baby should become a victim of abortion. My name is called now, my fate is going to be determined. Weight, fine; height, a little under average; pulse, fine; last period; ultrasound... I'm seven months pregnant. Mom is crying. Shoot, I'm crying too.

The last two months: I'm so mad, sad, and unhappy. Miserable. I wonder what I will do.

Fast forward. She's here, she is Kmiyah. I love her. She is a lot like me. She is so jolly, and she's my everything. I never give up. I'll never tell her she's a mistake, and I'll never tell her she held me back, because she never once asked to be here.

I admit, sometimes it gets hard. I worry about what tomorrow will bring. Sometimes I wonder: Am I good enough? I took on a big responsibility, because I am still a kid myself. Sometimes I have to sacrifice my hairdo for her diapers, or my getting my nails done for her new shoes. It's hard. No one told me life would be easy. I am on the route to change.

There is a line I love by the singer Vivian Greene: "Life isn't about waiting for the storm to pass, it's about learning to dance in the rain." I learned to dance in the rain. I am now a ninth grader attending Chicago Talent Development High School and I am doing fine. However, Kmiyah and especially I will never forget the experience I had being pregnant and giving birth at such a very young age. For me, though, that's all history, and never once have I looked back and blamed my beautiful baby girl or myself for what happened.

AFTER-SCHOOL TUTORING *and* WRITING

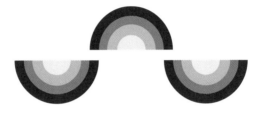

Monday through Thursday, from 3:00ᴘᴍ to 5:30ᴘᴍ, 826CHI is packed with students attending the after-school tutoring program. Our volunteer tutors are ready and waiting to help them with whatever homework they may have, from spelling words to Algebra to the occasional report on the long-tailed weasel.

When students arrive for after-school tutoring, they visit the 'Writing Table' (fondly dubbed 'The Musical Banana' by one of our second graders, for reasons which remain unclear). Here, volunteers lead students in creative or expository writing activities for fifteen minutes before students begin to work on their homework. Encouraging students to write at the beginning of tutoring not only allows us to ensure that quality writing happens on a regular basis, but also provides students with an often-times much-needed creative break between learning at school and tackling homework (those weasels can really take it out of you).

While volunteers offer structured writing activities and prompts, students have the freedom to work on their own writing projects—and also to offer their own suggestions for prompts, such as "Would you rather have your mom or your grandma as your teacher?" or "Write about a world in which dogs can fly and monkeys can talk with a wind-talking language."

Once a month, students participate in 'revision week' where they work on perfecting a self-selected piece, which is then compiled into chapbooks to be shared with family, friends, and the world at large. In this section, you will find just a few of the many stories and poems created each day at the Writing Table.

A Wig If You Want It

BY Bryan Montalban, *Grade 4*
FROM *Where the Wild Thanks Are, Fall 2009*

My MONSTER DOES whatever I say. Sometimes I tell him to feed me. He knows how to read and write, and he can do math, social studies, and science. He can help me with everything I have trouble with, like my homework, finishing chores, and making furniture. My monster can help me because he is smart at everything. His name is Mike Resource.

If you are evil, my monster blasts you with his fire blaster on his legs. Then he flies with his turbo jets, which help him reach super speed. He can shoot lasers out of his eyes if he doesn't close his eyes.

My monster looks like he can blend into anything. He is red and blue. He is big. He has two legs and a fire blaster on one hand and the other hand is a wig dispenser. He puts you in a wig if you want it, because some people do not like their hair, so they want to replace it.

Mexico

BY Cristian Rodriguez, *Grade 2*
FROM *Half Cold, Half Not, Winter 2009*

If I go to Mexico, I will see my
Grandma.

I will ride a horse and a donkey
and get a cowboy suit.

She is going to let me touch her
chickens

and cows.

Blending Wite-Out

BY Paula Mendez, *Grade 6*
FROM *Mini Monster on the Moon, Fall 2009*

DON'T YOU HATE IT when you use Wite-Out and it comes out a mess, not to mention how horrible it smells or how the roll-on kind doesn't stick on the paper, or how you can't curve it?

Well, now you don't have to go through all of that trouble! I have invented a new Wite-Out! It is not just plain white—it's see-through. Now, when you use it, it won't come out as big blobs, and it will stick right on to the paper.

With this Wite-Out, you can also curve the lines however you want. You don't have to pick it up to start a new line to erase, you just have to curve it!

I've thought about this before, a couple of weeks ago, when I was drawing something with a pen on a colored sheet of paper, which was not my best idea. I made a mistake and thought about how it would be so cool if the Wite-Out could blend in to the paper to correct my mistake.

Then, *TA-DA!* I wanted to make it real, and someday I will.

The best reason to use my Wite-Out will be because it will smell nothing like the old Wite-Out—it will smell like vanilla!

Thoughts on Pluto

BY Esmeralda Miranda, *Grade 5*
FROM *Mini Monster on the Moon, Fall 2009*

IF I COULD BE FROM PLUTO or Mars, I would want to be from
Pluto. I would like to be from Pluto because the scientists
say that Pluto is not a planet. I want to see for myself if
that's true. When I do figure it out, I'll prove the scientists
wrong! I think everyone's being mean to Pluto, and I want to
stop it.

A Triangle You Can Eat:
A Haiku

BY Fabian Felix, *Grade 3*
FROM *Half Cold, Half Not, Winter 2009*

I like cheese pizza:
a triangle you can eat.
The sauce tastes so good.

Carlo's Weird Day

BY Jennifer Resendiz, *Grade 4*
FROM *Meauh Shakes & Milk Sharks, Winter 2010*

WHEN CARLO WOKE UP, he opened the window and saw that teachers and dogs, cats and parents were randomly outside. They threw eggs at him. He went into the bathroom to take a shower. When he grabbed the shampoo, he opened it and orange liquid came out with little pieces of ham in it. He turned on the water and yellow liquid come out of the faucet. Carlo was surprised. Then, he went to brush his teeth and four teeth came out.

Carlo went to school and lots of kids laughed at him. He was sad. It was lunchtime and he ate a hamburger. When he looked at it, there was a mole on it with hair. Then, Carlo went home and went to sleep.

When Carlo went to sleep, he did not notice the fifty cats beside him. All fifty cats scratched him on his cheek. The cats were from each state in the United States.

Suddenly, a kid came through Carlo's window and slapped him. The kid jumped back out the window. All the cats scratched him at the same time. Carlo thought, "What just happened?"

Carlo went to the kitchen and ate a slice of ham and he exploded. When he exploded, things went back to normal.

His girlfriend came over and said, "Will you marry me?"

Carlo thought, *I am not going to marry you!*

His girlfriend thought, *Yes.* But she just told him, "Okay, Carlo, don't worry."

Carlo jumped rope, fell, and broke his leg. He went to the hospital and the doctor said, "You've been eating too much ham."

What is Mona L. Looking At?

BY Joel Cornelius, *Grade 8*
FROM *Half Cold, Half Not, Winter 2009*

I THINK MONA L. was looking at a mirror. She was watching herself pose. Also, she was watching Leonardo da Vinci draw her.

Da Vinci was drawing her because he was her long-lost brother. He was her twin brother that had been secretly adopted by another person. Their mother never knew.

They met at a mirror convention. They each thought they were looking into a funny mirror. They were looking at each other. Da Vinci drew a portrait of her because he wanted to draw a picture of himself. Mona L. wanted a portrait of herself, too, so she agreed.

Vanilla Milkshake

BY José "BJ" Antolin, Jr., *Grade 3*
FROM *Meauh Shakes and Milk Sharks, Winter 2010*

O, vanilla milkshake, you are sweet and salty
and you have chunks of lava in you.
But I drank you anyway.
You burned my mouth and all of my teeth.
My teeth melted and it tasted gross and the lava mixed
with my acid and the lava went out of my body and I hurled
really bad.
Happy Birthday, milkshake.

An Unrecorded Story

BY Alta Aegisdottir, *Grade 5*
FROM *Alta's 826CHI Writing Journal, Winter 2010*

ON A HARD SHELF I sat, my head touching my legs. I wished the nurse had put me down more comfortably. My china face was pale and my hair was almost white, my light blue dress was in an awful position and my black leather shoes were untied.

"The nurse ought to be punished," I thought bitterly. If I had only someone to talk to, I might have had a better time on 19th Cole Street, West Avenue, but neither could I talk nor did I have someone I dared to talk with.

It was not as terrible as I thought when it happened on the hard shelf of 19th Cole Street, West Avenue. I always knew that it would happen, just not this way. The nurse pushed me out of the way to place a teddy bear where I had so uncomfortably been placed. I fell far down and crushed into the Swedish carpet that lay on the floor like a rectangular pancake.

I remember nothing except the nurse's scream until I woke up on a wooden stool with a cushion, with glue all over my china face.

"Ew," I thought with disgust as a drop of glue ran down my face. Soon my lips were being repainted and so were my eyes. I must say, though, that I refuse to get glue on my face again.

How to Dance With a Robot

BY Mason Hammond, *Grade 5*
FROM *Sinks Covered in Foam, Spring 2009*

IF YOU EVER DANCE with a robot—which I highly recommend
you don't—you ought to mirror every move the robot makes.
The robot's favorite dance is the very popular hip-hop move
known as the "Robot": a series of stiff movements of arms
and legs finishing with the "Wave".

- The robot points its fingers up, having the wrist
  correspond.
- The elbow bends in a 120° angle while the shoulder
  follows.
- The fingers loop in a downward motion while the
  wrist is at a 90° angle with the palm. At the same
  time this is happening, the robot's elbows should be
  straightening out.

- Once its arm is entirely straightened out, the elbow should be turned over so it points to the sky and the forearm drops.
- Energy is transferred through its chest to its other arm where the motions repeat.
- At the end of the dance, both arms form 90° angles at the shoulders, letting the forearm sway.

PLEASE NOTE: Robots usually dance the "Robot", but on occasion they may do the "Limbo" or the "Conga Line". Typically, robots dance at a rate of 90bpm to 120bpm (beats per minute). At the end of the "Robot", robots may move their forearms slightly from side-to-side but enough so that you are able to see it move. This is how they wave at the end of the dance. They also incorporate a shuffle step.

Sarah's Poem Has No Title

BY Sarah Meyer, *Grade 8*
FROM *Half Cold, Half Not, Winter 2009*

Swinging, hanging,
dangling in the air.
Innocence.

Smiling, laughing,
staring at the sky.
Adolescence.

Until we grow up,
we'll be here.
Swinging in the air,
laughing at the skies.

Subservient:
to no one.
((Except ourselves))
Innocence.

How About a Turtle?

BY Brennan Klaassen, *Grade 6*
FROM *Tales of Talking Rooms, Mythic Creatures, and Cheeseburger Attacks, Fall 2009*

Dear Gimli,

Are you the main dwarf in *Lord of the Rings?* I hope so. Otherwise, please pass this on to the correct Gimli.

I was wondering, do you have Halloween? If you don't, throw this letter away. But anyway, I have an idea for a costume. I was watching your splendid performance in *The Two Towers* and I noticed that, with that shield on your back, you looked like a turtle. All you would need is a mask and you could go on all fours. You would also need a little paint on your shield and on your arms and legs. By the way, how many pounds do you weigh? I'm not being offensive. If you want, you could be a snapping turtle. At Wal-mart they have

an expensive turtle head that cuts into steel with the beak.
It costs about $300.

Sincerely,
Brennan K.

Snow

BY Adriana Castrillón, *Grade 6*
FROM *Meauh Shakes and Milk Sharks, Winter 2010*

Snow is cold and
soft
like an autumn breeze,
except it's freezing.
It's cold.
It turns my hands pink
but I don't think about it
much. I just focus on winning
the snowball fight.
Snow is soft and light—
it's nice and in a way,
it's bright against the
dull, gray
sky.

Aisle 2

BY Jillian Hutton, *Grade 5*
FROM *Mini Monster On the Moon, Fall 2009*

ONCE THERE WAS a broom named Kid who lived in Aisle 2 of the grocery store. Kid wanted to be a penguin. He wanted to be a penguin because he loved penguins—where they lived, it was nice and cool, and the island was made out of flavored shaved ice you could eat.

Kid went to fishing school, which taught both fishing and regular school like math and spelling and reading and science and social studies. He was going so he could learn how to fish because his dad was a fisherman and he wanted Kid to do what he did. Fishing ran in the family.

"My dad was a fisherman," Kid's dad said, "and his dad was a fisherman. And so on, and so on."

Kid's mom was a scientist, and she studied micro-animals in the oceans, seas, and other bodies of water. Things like fungus, too.

Every morning, she would say to kid, "Have a good day at school by the water." After school, when Kid got home, he would lay down on the couch with a big *ufflll* sound, and his mother would ask, "What was it like at fishing school by the water? Did you see any micro-animals?"

One day at his fishing school, Kid's teacher asked, "Do you know what 6x6 is?" and he said, "Yes."

"Then what is it?"

"36," he answered.

Suddenly, a kid named Nerdy Ferdy started to talk to the broccoli trees, who were outside hanging in the ice cream shop, where they were eating cookies 'n' cream, twist, and chocolate-and-peanut butter ice cream.

He said, "I'm eleven years old and I have two people in my family."

The broccoli trees said in a sassy voice, "Why would we need to know that?"

The nerd replied, "I thought you wanted to go out with me?"

"In your dreams!" said the broccoli trees.

There was a girl that Kid knew. Her name was Celery. Celery liked mac 'n' cheese out of the box. She had a brother named Pea who was older and washed cars for a living. She also had a sister named Corn who chopped down trees for a living. Celery also had a mom and a dad who were writers and liked to write about animals and wildlife. Celery dreamed about being an athlete who won medals and received awards.

One day, Celery got into a cart with Kid and went to the ice cream aisle to eat some ice cream. Then they went to the freezer aisle and got some water and put it on the floor. Kid and Celery froze the water and started to skate on the ice, eating ice cream out of the cartons at the same time. They were doing circles and swerves and the two of them were really happy.

At the end of the day, they went to go watch the sunset in the valley. When the sun set, Kid and Celery looked at each other and got closer and closer until their lips touched. After that, they just looked back at the sunset, feeling happy and weird, blushing.

Forest

BY Amanda Miranda, *Grade 8*
FROM *Mini Monster on the Moon, Fall 2009*

FAR AWAY FROM HOME, somewhere out beyond, lies this poor
forest. Everything seems dead, but it's rebuilding. In the
morning, there are many trees, green as ever. There isn't any
grass to be found, just a lot of stumps and trees. The stumps
aren't nice and flat, they point up. You don't want to sit on
these stumps, skinny and tall trees with not so many leaves.
Everything is wet. (No, not really, maybe only the ground.) I
don't think you want to sit anywhere in this forest. Better
yet, don't come out.

AT-LARGE SUBMISSIONS

While we have had the good fortune to work with thousands of young writers at 826CHI, we are also excited to include the writing of several students throughout the Chicago area who have sent us their own submissions.

We welcome writers ages 6 to 18 to join our ranks by submitting work of which they are especially proud to our next publication. These submissions may or may not include essays, poetry, short stories, lyrics, news articles, comics, reviews, lists, character sketches, journal entries, instructions, interviews, opinion articles, reconnaissance findings, memoirs, missives, declarations, plays, graphic novels, fables, factoids pertaining to the long-tailed weasel, limericks, jokes, gardening tips, odes, gross exaggerations, sound advice, exceptionally good recipes for chocolate chip muffins, and flights of fancy.

If you have written something along these lines, or along any other type of line for that matter, email your submission, with your full name, age, and school to publications@826chi.org. If you prefer to send regular mail, telegram, or carrier pigeon, our address is:

826CHI
Attn: Publications
1331 North Milwaukee Avenue
Chicago, Illinois 60622

A Collaboration

BY Samantha Celmer and Kalila Holt, *Grade 11*

To be read in an English accent.

153

THERE WAS A KNOCK at the door. Galileo put down his toast and went to answer it. He shuffled to the foyer in his tattered bunny slippers grumbling, "Terribly inconvenient time for someone to just stop by. I'm eating my toast right now."

He grabbed his rusty old doorknob and shook it violently until the door gave way.

"Oh, Jesus," he sighed upon seeing Tyraneus on the doorstep, looking bright-eyed and cheery.

"Hello, my good friend," Tyraneus bellowed. "Isn't it quite the perfect morning for a hunt?"

"No," snapped Galileo. "I don't believe it is. I believe it's the perfect morning for eating toast without Tyraneus."

AT-LARGE SUBMISSIONS

"Oh, you old devil," he laughed, thinking it a joke. "You know those tricky little scoundrels won't eradicate themselves. Now be a good chap, and put on those nice pants I bought you. They are perfect for attracting those confounded squirrels."

Galileo had tried to throw the pants in his electric fireplace when Tyraneus had first given them to him. As a result, they were badly singed and even more unattractive than they had been initially.

"Oh dear, old chap," Tyraneus chuckled upon Galileo's return from the closet. "I do hope you remembered to stop, drop, and roll!"

"Umm, yes," Galileo mumbled. "That's exactly what I did. Perhaps I shouldn't wear them since they are in such a condition."

"Pish posh!" cried Tyraneus. "These pants are essential to our craft!"

"Alright," Galileo responded quite sadly. His hopes for an uneventful morning had been dashed. He dragged himself into his floral bathroom and changed out of his mallard pajamas into the tight, silver, metallic pants. Oh, how he hated those dreadful pants!

"What took you so long? Did you fall into the loo? Ha ha! Well, have you done both your mental and physical exercises to prepare for our expedition? Or do I have to go over them with you again?"

"Oh no," Galileo assured him. "I've been working on those all morning."

Tyraneus seemed not to hear him and situated himself comfortably by the window. As the unwanted guest screamed "*SQUIRREL!*" whenever he saw one of the wretched creatures, Galileo thought back to how he first came to be involved in such a strange activity. It was his fortieth birthday, he recalled. Almost twelve years ago. He'd just recently moved to Granberg, a small suburb forty minutes outside of Bath. He was sitting at home, eating some toast, when he noticed a strange man hiding in the bushes outside his house.

"Ey! What do you think you're doing?" he asked as he leaned his head out the window.

"Ho there!" exclaimed the lurker. "Good morrow, old chap! Care to assist me in ridding the world of its vermin?"

Galileo flinched. "You don't have to talk so loudly. I'm rather close, you see. And what do you mean?"

"What do I mean!" said the man, just as loudly. "Don't you know who I am? I am Tyraneus the Great!"

"Are you part of the royal family or something?" Galileo asked as he thought of the rumors about the Queen having a mentally unbalanced nephew.

"Perhaps, but the MI6 have gotten rid of any proof of that, those fiendish mongrels. And what is your name, old chap?"

"Galileo," he answered.

"Ha ha HA!" laughed Tyraneus. "Shall I drop something on your head so you can discover gravity?"

"That wasn't Galileo," Galileo tried to tell him.

"Of course it was, of course it was!" insisted Tyraneus. "So then, are you ready? Or would you like to change into something more appropriate?"

"More appropriate for what?"

"The great quest, my lad! The most noble mission of them all!"

"Which is?" grumbled Galileo, who did not appreciate being called "my lad" on his fortieth birthday.

"Which *is*? Which is! You ask as if you don't know. Ha! You sly fellow, you. Squirrel hunting, of course!"

To this day, Galileo could not remember what exactly was said to make him agree to such an absurd pastime. Perhaps it was the only thing he could do to appease the man, perhaps there was bribery involved, or perhaps it was the loneliness that he pretended he did not feel. All he knew was that here he was, on what would have been a perfectly lovely morning, crouching in the bushes in burnt metallic pants with a man who spoke too loudly.

After so many years of failing to catch the "tricky scoundrels," as Tyraneus liked to call them, they were going to try something new.

"What in the name of England are those for?" asked Galileo suspiciously as Tyraneus unearthed two fishing poles.

"What do you think?" boomed Tyraneus. "Squirrel catching! It's a new tactic!"

With difficulty, he tried to shove an acorn onto the hook. It did not work, and instead the acorn went flying out of his hand and hit Galileo on the head. Tyraneus laughed as

156

Galileo took off the hook and tied the stem of the acorn to the pole.

"There," he said, his face red with embarrassment. "Now, go on then. Let's get this over with."

"Fore!" Tyraneus yelled, casting the bait out onto the lawn.

"Now what?" Galileo asked.

"Well," Tyraneus explained. "One of those tricky scoundrels will see the bait and start to come towards it. As it gets closer, we slowly—very slowly—pull it towards this acorn-filled cage." He pulled the cage of Galileo's dead canary, Roger, out of a bush.

"Where did you get that from?" he cried, outraged.

"No matter. Now! Hush hush, I see one coming across the lawn."

There was, in fact, a squirrel on the lawn. It ran by without even pausing to look at the acorn.

"That one was blind. I'm sure of it! The next one, I tell you. The next one," Tyraneus said, and he continued to say it for the next hour and a half.

"I didn't know there was a blind squirrel epidemic," said Galileo sarcastically.

"Oh yes, I believe it has to do with the water supply," assured Tyraneus. "You know, old chap, there are several fountains with—"

"Shut your trap, you old fool!" interrupted Galileo. "Look!"

Out on the grass, a squirrel, whose vision was apparently in perfect working order, had stopped to examine the acorn. Tyraneus began to reel in the bait.

"Slowly! Slowly!" whispered Galileo, who was actually excited for the first time in his life.

"Easy, old chap," replied Tyraneus. "I've got this little scroundrel."

The squirrel followed the acorn across the lawn, closer to the bushes. "Go," Galileo whispered. "Go. Go. *Go, go, go!*"

And go he did. He peeked his tiny rodent head into the cage, deemed it satisfactory, and hopped in.

"Hurrah!" bellowed Tyraneus, slamming the cage shut. "We've done it, old chap! We've done it!"

They smiled like old fools and gave each other manly pats on the back. It was the first time Galileo had laughed since his eleventh birthday.

"Now what?" Galileo asked through chuckles, as he wiped tears from his eyes.

Tyraneus tried to hide his lack of expertise. "Well... well, now we... now we..."

They stared silently at the birdcage, which now contained a squirrel.

"Should we... should we let the old scoundrel go?" Tyraneus finally asked, ashamed.

"Yes," Galileo said. "I suppose we should."

"This is ridiculous," thought Galileo as they watched the idiot squirrel stumble out of the cage and run away. Even so, he found himself smiling for reasons he could not explain.

Waning

BY Claire Haffner, *Grade 12*

Thinning away to nothing
a shadow flickers in my bones
as the air thickens, weighing me down.

Eyes growing heavy with night,
I gorge myself on hope,
but it's never enough—
always fading before I savor the last bite.

My threadbare thoughts
and fraying feelings
pull me into the gentle sea of apathy,
and I find there's air
beneath the surface.

The Explosion of Spaceship #7

BY Lawrie L. Zhang, *Grade 5*

ADA LOT HURRIED EXCITEDLY into the spaceship parking lot with her two sisters Idaline and Ella Lot. Today, Ada, Idaline, and Ella, the triplets, were going on a spaceship tour that would last seven days! Ella had suggested the idea, and since it was educational, and it was Christmas, their parents scraped up enough money to buy them each a spaceship ticket as their Christmas present.

As they approached the spaceship, Ada gripped onto her metallic ticket until her knuckles turned white. They walked through the white December snowflakes and approached the man in front of the spaceship.

"Tickets, please," the man said.

Each girl slid her metal ticket through a slot, and then entered the spaceship. Inside, there were six million seats for passengers, forty seats for tour directors, and six seats for leaders and pilots. There was also a mini life-spaceship in the back, just in case of emergency.

As they sat down, the speaker announced, "PASSENGERS, PLEASE BUCKLE YOUR SEATBELTS."

Ada winced, covering her ears with her hands. "The speaker is so loud!" she complained.

"Whatever, Ada," Ella mumbled.

"Buckle your seatbelts!" Idaline snapped. Idaline was born one minute before Ella, and two minutes before Ada. This was why Idaline always acted bossy.

"You're not the boss, Ida!" Ada complained again, buckling her seatbelt quickly.

"Yeah, Ida!" Ella said crossly, buckling her seatbelt.

"I'm the oldest of the triplets, remember?" Idaline replied in a mocking voice.

"SPACESHIP #7 WILL NOW TAKE OFF!" The speaker announced, disrupting the triplets' argument.

All of a sudden, the spaceship blasted into the sky with super sonic speed.

"Yay, we're in the sky!" Idaline cheered.

"This is *awesome*!" Ella exclaimed.

A few minutes later, an eighteen-year-old girl entered the passengers' room. She had long, soft, curly, brown hair and dazzling emerald green eyes. She wore a name tag that read RAINA.

"Hi, guys. My name is Raina. I'm going to be your tour guide today," Raina began confidently. "We're going to pass by the sun first."

As they passed by the sun, Raina began explaining information and facts about it. Next, they passed by the moon. There were plenty of *ooo's* and *ahh's* as the passengers marveled at the sights.

The first day aboard the ship passed quickly. The next day, a man named Mr. Tim took over as a tour guide. As Mr. Tim talked about the Milky Way, Raina sat next to Ada, Ella, and Idaline.

"What are your names?" She asked after she was done reintroducing herself.

Ella spoke up. "I'm Ella. This is Ida, and this is Ada. We're non-identical, eleven-year-old triplets."

"My full name is Idaline," Idaline added triumphantly. "Isn't it unique?"

"Oh, whatever," Ella groaned, rolling her eyes.

"You guys are triplets? That's hard to believe. You look so different!" Raina exclaimed. Idaline had long, rough, straight, jet black hair that fell to her elbows and fiery, dark brown eyes. Ella had long, soft, curly blonde hair that went to the bottom of her arms and sparkly, bright blue eyes. Ada had long, silky, burgundy curls that reached her waist and calming, dark green eyes.

Ada winced. "I'm the laughingstock of the triplets because of my hair and eyes!" She cried.

"No you aren't. You're beautiful," Raina assured her.

"Are you sure?" Ada asked.

"You are, Ada," Ella said.

"You are beautiful and unique," Idaline added.

"Thanks," Ada smiled weakly.

"Now we're passing Venus," Mr. Tim announced.

"Venus? That's my favorite planet!" Ada exclaimed.

* * *

RAINA FELT LIKE SOMETHING was wrong. As she watched Ada, Ella, and Idaline having fun, a tiny bit of worry squeezed into her mind. She wasn't sure what was wrong, but she thought she'd better check it out in the pilot room.

"I'll be right back, guys," Raina told the triplets. She hurried into the pilot room as fast as she could.

"Hello there, Raina. How's it going?" Mr. Jay, one of the three pilots, greeted her.

"Hello, Mr. Jay. I'm just fine," Raina answered with a nervous smile. "I just wanted to make sure you guys were okay."

"Oh, we're doing marvelously!" Mr. Jay laughed.

"Oh, that's good. Well, then, see you..." Raina started to say goodbye to Mr. Jay when Mr. Prentiss, another pilot, screamed.

"*Helllp!*" He screamed. "Look!" He pointed outside.

Raina looked, and then froze, holding her breath. Another spaceship, Spaceship #6, had crashed into their ship!

"We're going to die!" Mr. Prentiss cried.

Raina began to panic. She rushed into the passengers' room and screamed as loudly as she could, "Our spaceship is going to EXPLODE!!!"

Within seconds, all the passengers were running around, screaming. A window shattered. Half of the spaceship destructed and fell into outer space. Passengers breathed shallowly, gasping for air. On the other half of the spaceship, millions of passengers lost their balance and fell into outer space, screaming. They disappeared into the dark.

Raina gasped, speechless in horror. Finally, she shouted to Mr. Jay, "Launch the life-spaceship!" The remaining passengers scrambled into the life-spaceship as quickly as they could.

"Come on, Raina!" Mr. Jay called.

Raina raced toward the life-spaceship. But before she could reach it, the floor beneath her slipped. The rest of the spaceship destructed and fell apart, then tumbled into outer space. Raina screamed as she fell with the remains of the spaceship. The life-spaceship flew away without her as she was swallowed by the darkness. Raina's mind spun around in total chaos, and she fell unconscious.

* * *

"Raina!" Ada cried desperately. "We have to save her!"

"You're right, Ada," Mr. Jay agreed. "Let's try to save her."

"But how?" Ella asked.

"I'll come up with a plan." Mr. Jay said, and with that, he sent the life spaceship diving down into the dark after Raina.

Raina opened her eyes. "Where am I?" She managed to choke out the words.

She heard a voice exclaim, "Raina is awake! She's alive!"

Raina suddenly remembered. She had slipped on the de-structed spaceship and she had fallen into outer space. She had fallen unconscious, but where was she now?

"Raina!" she heard the voice say again. Raina sat up, and then saw Ada.

"I'm in the life-spaceship?" Raina asked. "I don't believe this. Maybe it's a dream. I'm dead."

"No, it isn't a dream!" Ella quickly protested. "We rescued you! We caught you while you were falling!"

"How?" Raina asked, puzzled.

"Never mind that," Idaline said quickly. "We're landing on earth!"

* * *

The explosion of Spaceship #7 spread across the news every-where. Of course, many lives were lost and very few people dared to go on a spaceship ever again, but it was also an exciting event in history.

"Mom!" Ada cried, running towards Mrs. Lot.

"Oh, my daughters!" Mrs. Lot cried, giving each girl a squeeze. "You could've been killed!"

"We could've been," Idaline said, "but we weren't."

"I missed you!" Ella cried.

"Me, too!" cried Ada.

"Me, three!" Idaline joined in.

Each girl grinned as they went back to their family. Never again did they want to go on a spaceship!

* * *

"WELL, I GUESS I CAN work here, instead," Raina sighed as she entered Olive Garden. After a while, she earned her job there as a waitress. She also met a new friend named Lilly, another eighteen-year-old waitress at Olive Garden.

"Life's much better here than working as a tour guide on a spaceship, isn't it?" Lilly asked one day as they were taking their lunch break.

"It certainly is," Raina agreed, smiling. "It certainly is."

Fall Leaves An Impression

BY Ibrahim Ihmoud, *Grade 2*

It's cold outside

It's fall

The hail is cold

The trees are tall

Moving

It's windy

There are bees everywhere.

Do Not Touch

BY Ashley Dainas, *Recent High School Graduate*

IN A FIT OF NOSTALGIA for the good old days when hippies sang in parking lots and crazies chained themselves to trees, my mother dragged us, kicking and screaming, across seven counties to see the last piece of untouched land on Earth.

Really.

Sometimes I cannot help but feel that the woman stays up late most nights clutching a yellow legal pad and a red pen, cackling maniacally to herself as she thinks up ways to make her children miserable. Mommie Dearest, eat your heart out.

We're driving in the Navigator (our gas-guzzling life savior that only serves to highlight Mom's overbearing hypocrisy). Cally is sitting in the way back texting twenty friends at once. She's ten. Don't people talk anymore? Seriously. I'm fifteen, but sometimes I feel so freaking old I swear I can feel my skin sagging from my bones and my cholesterol skyrocketing.

Brendon and Jason are sitting next to me, miming all sorts of violent death scenes in an attempt to get mom to pull over and get some food. I watch disinterestedly as Jason stabs Brendon with a twelve-inch-long dagger. Brendon counters by pouring hot acid on Jason's face. Why couldn't my brothers be normal and play video games like ordinary brain dead children their age?

I miss Sarah. She's so lucky, all the way out there in Boston where none of this nonsense can reach her. I call her twice a week, though mom calls her every day. She always says she misses us. I glance around the gas-guzzler, noting the texting sister, mime-like brothers and red-faced mother cursing under her breath at the innocent pedestrians she just narrowly avoided hitting, and can't help but wonder. Why?

We arrive at a glorious green space off of Oakton and McCormick. We tromp out of the beast. Cally only leaves her phone in the car after a whispered WWIII between her and Mom. Mom won, obviously.

And then we see the sign.

It's white, with black lettering and corded off with yellow string and small red flags.

"Isn't it wonderful?" Mother cries, taking pictures (with the usual minor technical difficulties that Brendon always grudgingly solves).

"We came here for this?" Cally demands, turning around and plopping herself on the ground with a pretentious sniff.

"Are we done yet?" chorus the twins.

"Shut up," Mother replies lovingly.

And I?

What did I do when I saw the last piece of untouched land on Earth?

I reached down...

Poem #4

BY Sarah Siebuhr, *Grade 12*

i am bound to grow old,

become bitter,

fill with more sadness,

write poems in the third

person and beg the audience to become

a reader of high consequence, understand

that the brittle hand

gripping steering wheel

mouth still tasting like age

denying a cigarette

is not the poet, instead, speaker,

and you will ask:

how could i not love you back? and

what more is there to say?

the speaker is a husband is a wife when

a husband disappears, is gone
wife, audience, her senses hurt keen.
reader, a wife told a husband to build a life instead
with his hands and unexpected skin, languid
build me, she pleads.
never the poet.

Lumi Bright

BY Chandler Browne, *Grade 7*

PREFACE

THIS STORY IS ABOUT A BOY, who is a squid named Lumi. Lumi lives deep down at the bottom of the ocean, in a little town of about 1,000 squids. This town is named Deep Down Town. All of the squids in this town have bioluminescence, which means that they glow. They are a lot like us. They have a school and teachers and a principal. Even a coral driver named Hank. They have bullies and nerds and cheerleaders for the soccer team.

I hope you enjoy Lumi's story.

Chapter I

The Story Begins

SEPTEMBER 4TH IS THE DAY my life changed. It was the day that squids started to treat me with respect.

My story starts off on a normal day. At least it was normal for me—not everyone gets teased and messed with every day. You see, I have a very rare, non-medical condition. I have non-bioluminescence. This means that I do not have bioluminescence. This may not seem big, but it is out of the ordinary for our kind. Everyone else at the bottom of the ocean glows. Sunlight can't reach down here, so we use other energy sources from other places. When ships pass overhead or sink, they leave behind many resources that we can use. Our science teacher, Mr. H_2O, taught us how to use these resources to our advantage.

So, let me tell you about September 4th.

Chapter II

That Morning

IT WAS THE DAY I had been dreading all summer, the first day back to school. It wasn't my first day at a new school or anything like that. I didn't have the symptoms that a normal boy squid would have on the first day at a new year of school. I didn't have butterflies in my stomach, nor did I spend all morning practicing what I would say. In fact, I had no intention of actually attending school. But then I heard my mom.

"Get out of bed," my mom demanded.

"Five more minutes," I moaned.

"Fine, but you can only have until the timer rings for breakfast, and, as soon as it does, I want your tentacles on that floor and I want you to march down those coral steps."

As soon as she was done demanding, that stupid timer rang.

"Would you look at that? That is just fate if you ask me," my mom said.

"I didn't ask you anything," I said under my breath.

"What did you say?" she demanded.

"Nothing," I moaned.

"That's what I thought," she said happily.

I slowly slid out of bed, dreading each movement. Why did it have to be *me*? Why did *I* have to be the one who got stuffed in the lockers with not a glimpse of light? Why did *I* have to be me, the only squid in history that didn't glow?

"Hurry up. I have a back-to-school surprise for you downstairs," Mom said.

"Really? I hope it includes not having to go."

"If it included you not going, it wouldn't be a back-to-school surprise, now would it?"

"I guess not, but I'd rather not go and get no present than go and get a present," I explained.

"Well, you're still going whether you want to or not."

"Fine."

Once I got downstairs, I saw some weird, giant piece of headgear on the kitchen table. It had some sort of flashlight that came from a sunken ship. It had a ribbon, crossed and sewn together securely in the shape of the letter "T." The flashlight was attached somehow to the ribbon. I hadn't even noticed the worst part yet. There was a lemon attached at the top by some wires.

"What is this?" I said fiercely.

"It's your surprise," she said casually.

"I figured that. But what exactly is it?"

"It's a flashlight attached to a ribbon. I found the parts when I was taking your sister to day care. I made it so you would be able to see the next time you get lost or stuffed into a locker."

"What's the lemon for?" I asked.

"The light didn't work so I had to get the electricity from the lemon."

"Oh. Okay."

I have forgotten to tell you another disadvantage to having non-bioluminescence. I get lost a lot after school.

"I can't wear that to school. They don't allow hats."

"It's not a hat," Mom replied.

I didn't want to actually tell her the truth: That weird piece of headgear would give Bob (the school's biggest bully) another reason to mess with me.

Mom had gotten her way, as usual.

"Well, fine," I said, giving up.

"You'll wear it," she said in a higher octave than normal.

"If you insist."

"Good," she insisted.

"Uhhhhh, sure."

She put breakfast on the table and gave me a fork.

"Finish up that food fast or you'll be late."

"I want to be late."

"Don't be smart with me, Luminescence."

My whole name is "Luminescence." It's kind of weird that my name means light, and I can't even make a faint spark. Not only does my name not suit me in any way whatsoever, my mom only calls me by my full name when she is angry with me or I'm being a nuisance. Compelling stuff, huh?

"Hellllllooooo, you're not even listening to me." Apparently she was lecturing me while my mind was drifting off on a different subject.

"Yeah, I was," I lied.

"No, you weren't," she said.

"Yes, I was."

"Okay. Then what did I say?"

"Ummmmmm..."

"That's what I thought," she said. "Go to school. You don't want to be later than you already are."

"Yes, I do."

I started to head out the door when she called me back.

"Luminescence, you forgot your present."

I grabbed it and started to head out again.

"Aren't you going to put it on?"

I didn't say anything. I just strapped it on my head. The last thing I wanted to do was hurt her feelings.

"Bye," I said trying to keep the real expression—that should have been on my face—off it.

"Good luck," she said with a smile.

I was going to need lots of good luck—more like a miracle —even to have a decent day at school.

Chapter III

First Day Back

Everyone looked the same, even our principal, Mr. Sourpuss. When the bell rang, everyone went to their classes, except of course for the bully of all bullies, Bob. Most people at school called him "Bob the Bully." I think he liked the name.

As soon as I happened to notice him, he barely—but enough—happened to notice me. He started to swim over to me, probably to make remarks about my newly found headgear.

Maybe I could find an escape route. Nope. Just my luck. Every possible escape route was gone. All students were safely in their classrooms. I, on the other hand, was all alone in the hallway. Except for one squid, Bob the Bully.

"Hey, Squirt!" He looked like he'd been looking forward to saying that all summer.

"Howdy."

"So, look what we have here—a loser with a lemon on his head."

I didn't say anything.

"So, what time suits your schedule for our annual black-eye meeting?"

I didn't make a sound. I just stood there.

"How's after school? Four-fifteen sharp."

I stood silently and swallowed.

"Good. I'm looking forward to it."

Neither he nor I said anything else. He just shoved me into a locker.

"Four-fifteen *sharp*. Don't be late." With that, he slammed the locker door shut.

When I finally managed to get out of that locker, I went to class.

Class was class, boring as always. In Science we talked about the cells of different species, in Writing we talked about irregular verbs and how nasty they can be, in Social Studies we talked about the first king of the Square Table, and in Math we did algebra (ugh!). And my fellow students got a good laugh out of my new headgear.

When school was finished at four o'clock, I started to shake, scared of what might happen soon. Before I knew it, it was four-fifteen. I kept shaking and almost fell down. Bob saw me and swam up. When he was about a yard away from me, he said, "So... You look frantic."

I was hoping that my panicked heartbeat would not show up on my face. So much for that!

"I, um..." I sounded just like I looked. Frantic.

"So, how about we go around the corner and have a casual conversation?"

"Ummmmmm..." I couldn't say any real words. Usually when Bob says "let's have a casual conversation," it's code for "let's go around the corner so I can beat you up." But maybe, just maybe, he meant what he said, and we would just be having a conversation. But my chances were very, very slim.

"Good. We can talk about today's wrestling match."

We both knew that there was no wrestling match. We both also knew that he was talking about the wrestling match that was about to happen, the one where he would beat me up.

As he pulled me around the corner, he said, "So, I see your mom finally noticed how much of a disappointment you are. She finally got you something to help your disability." He put great effort into insulting me. It worked.

All of a sudden I felt a hard shove in the middle of my body. I fell over. Bob snatched my headgear and crushed the flashlight with his tentacles. My lemon-powered, flashlight headgear was destroyed. And, as much as I had hated it, I wished that Bob hadn't smashed it. My mom had made it for me, and I wanted it back. I got mad—really mad—and so I ran toward him with all of my might and punched him. He didn't even flinch. He looked like he hadn't even felt it. Bob just started to laugh.

"That was entertaining," Bob sneered.

Then, to add insult to injury, Bob inked me. (For those of you who don't know, squids can shoot black ink out of their backsides.) Yuck!!! I was covered in Bob's ink!

"See ya' round, loser," Bob snickered as he turned away and swam off.

Chapter IV
Cloria

After our "conversation" was over, I started to head home, dripping black ink all the way. And, not to my surprise, I got lost. I was not paying attention to where I was going. And I did not have my headgear to light my way.

It wasn't until I ran headfirst into a rock that I realized just how lost I was. I found a good place to sit down and I sulked. I must tell you that I shed a few tears.

All of a sudden, I saw a slight glow. I was positive it was not me, so it had to be someone else. Maybe Bob had come to mess with me again. But I hadn't heard tentacle steps or swishes of any kind. The only thing I heard was a slight humming sound. Curiously, wiping my nose, I looked up. There was what seemed to be a mermaid. I had only seen pictures of mermaids in books, not in actual life. They usually stayed 3,500 feet below sea level. They *never* came this far down to the bottom of the ocean.

"Lumi," she said slowly with a very kind voice. "Lumi, don't be upset."

"What in the world?" I said to myself.

"Oh, how rude of me. My name is Cloria," she said.

But I was still scared so I picked up a stick. "Stay back! I have a stick!"

"I can see that," she answered.

"What do you want? I have nothing to give you."

"It is not what you can do for me. It's what I can do for you."

"What?"

"I can give you one wish... but only one."

"Why do you want to grant me a wish?" I threw down the stick.

"Because I can see that you are sad, and I want to help."

"I learned about your kind in school," I said. "Mermaids can't live this far down."

"So?"

"So? So you should be suffocating right now because of the pressure."

"I have my ways."

"What kinds of ways are those?"

"Do you want your wish or not?" She started to sound annoyed.

"No," I answered.

Taken aback, she said, "Okay, but I think you'll regret your decision."

She was about to swim away when I changed my mind.

"Wait!!!! I want my wish, Cloria," I shouted.

She stopped. "That's what I thought. So, what shall your wish be? The end of global warming? Peace on Earth? To be the richest living organism? What?"

"I want Bob the Bully to get back what he has been dishing out to me all these years."

"Oh, well, are you sure? You only get one wish."

"Yes, I'm positive."

"Okay then."

With a snap of her fingers, she was gone. Better yet, to my utter surprise, I was standing just outside of my house. Because it all seemed too good to be true, I said to myself, "Probably just some prank." I swam inside, washed off the rest of Bob's ink, ate dinner, and went to bed.

Chapter V

One Great Day

When I got to school the next day, everyone was happy, talking about how Bob had gotten beaten up by some new girl. I couldn't believe what I was hearing so I had to see it for myself. Everyone said that he was in the cafeteria. When I got to the cafeteria, there he was... with a repulsive black eye.

"This isn't over, Cloria!" he yelled.

"Wanna bet?" Cloria yelled back.

Cloria? Did he say Cloria? It couldn't be the same mermaid? Here at school? How was this possible?

She winked at me and then swam out.

"What are *you* looking at?" Bob asked me all, embarrassed.

"Me? Are you talking to me?"

"No. Duh."

"No one. I was looking at nobody."

He slowly swam around me and left.

I couldn't believe my wish had come true. Bob the Bully had gotten justice. This was going to be great!

Next day, Bob got beaten up again, and then the next, and then the next. The next time I saw him, he looked awful. He had deep purple bruises and another repulsive black eye. He could barely swim. For some reason, I felt horrible. Bob had never beaten me up that badly. Nobody deserved to be beaten up like that. I had to get Cloria to take back the wish.

Chapter VI

Take It Back

The following day, I looked for Cloria high and low, low and high, until I found her. She was at lunch with her newly-found gang of worshippers. I swam over to her.

"Can I speak to you, please?" I asked.

"You'll have to excuse me," she said to her worshippers.

We swam over to another part of the cafeteria.

"I want you to take back the wish."

"Why?" She looked at me as though I was out of my mind.

"Because it's just not right."

"Why do you care? He deserves it. Putting you through all of that bullying. Boys like that deserve punishment."

"Well, you're just as bad. Maybe even worse. He never beat me up so badly."

"Even if that's true, I can't take it back," Cloria said.

"You need to take it back."

"I can't."

"Why not?"

"Because I don't have the power to."

"Then who does?"

"Only the rarest of the starfish can break the wish."

"What are you talking about?"

"What I'm talking about is you finding a Mitochondria Starfish and wishing on it."

"Where can I find one of *those*?"

"I'm not exactly sure, but I think you can find them in the town Cytoplasm."

"And where might that be?"

She just shrugged her shoulders and swam away.

Chapter VII

Perfect Timing

On the way home, I kept trying to figure out how I would ever find a Mitochondria Starfish or the town called Cytoplasm. Since I was so deep in thought, once again, I got lost. I began swimming in circles and wished I still had my flashlight headgear. At just about the same time that I found my bearings, I noticed something in my peripheral vision. Something blue, starfish blue. And there was exactly what I needed—a Mitochondria Starfish.

Like me, he seemed to be lost.

"Are you lost?" I asked.

"Yes and no."

"What do you mean by yes and no?"

"Well, I know where I am going, just not how to get there."

"Can I help?"

"Sure. I'm trying to get home. I live in small town called Cytoplasm. Have you ever heard of it?"

"Yes, I've heard of it, but I don't know how to get there. Sorry."

"Thank you, kind young squid, for the thought. It's the thought that counts. Is there anything I can do for you? Anything at all?"

"Well, there is this one thing. I was wondering if you could take back a wish I made with a mermaid."

"If you don't mind me asking, what did you wish for?"

I told him the entire story, every little detail. How Bob messed with me because I didn't glow, how I made the wish and it got out of hand, how I was going to search high and low to find a Mitochondria Starfish just when I met him.

"Why do you care what happens to Bob?" the starfish asked. "The way you make it sound, he deserves it."

"'Cause, well, I guess I learned that when I did what he did to me, back to him, I was no better than he is. Maybe even worse."

"Come again?"

"Well, I realized that, if I'm a bully, I'm not any better than he is."

"Ah, you learned a lesson. And fast. It would take most young squids much longer to figure that out. You will be great one day." He sounded proud of my realization.

"Thank you. Will you help me?"

"Of course. It has already been done."

"Really?"

"Yes."

"Thank you. You have no idea what this means."

Epilogue

Sure enough, there were no more fights. Cloria did not show up at school again, and Bob never messed with me again. I guess he learned his lesson, too. From that day forward, I was known and respected for who I am, "Luminescence Bright."

The Flat-Faced Boy

By Zoe Netter, *Grade 10*

THE FLAT-FACED BOY rarely spoke. When he did allow words to escape, their preciousness made a simple ham-sandwich-and-a-Coke-please sound like a spiritual revelation—deep, quiet words weighted just enough by percussive consonants to keep them floating at eye level several minutes after they had been spoken.

His words always frightened the bed-headed woman, who was particularly on edge at the moment, attempting to pick a lock with a bent-up bobby pin.

Are you sure this is a good idea? flat-faced boy asked.

Bed-headed woman jumped and dropped the pin, her stubby fingers trembling. The right hand fumbled for another pin while the left hand guarded her fluttering heart.

Don't do that to me. Bent down, her nose barely reached his belly button, but the stench of authority and too much perfume carried her message up to his gangly world. The flat-faced boy said nothing. He watched as pearly hail pellets collected on the bed-headed woman's coat, struggling to pick the lock on the door.

The door finally gave way and the bed-headed woman pushed through into the shadowed house. She knew the flat-faced boy would wait outside, his large protruding ears turning deeper and deeper shades of pink in the cold. There would be no words offering help. She routinely did this part alone. After much drawer-opening, pillow-lifting, and nightstand-shifting she found what she was looking for and stashed it under her bulky black coat.

Bed-headed woman waddled through the front door and beckoned to the flat-faced boy, who gently closed the door before following small boot prints down the creaky porch steps. He smiled. The flat-faced boy and the bed-headed woman lumbered and toddled home. Home was where iron fence posts no longer stood rigid guard but bent backwards, as if to sit, or forward, with pelvises thrust out in a lazy stretch. Home was where customers no longer flocked to darkened shop windows. Only dead leaves and old Styrofoam cups took any interest in the dusty displays. Home was the pizza-faced, graffiti-tattooed apartment building that was always full of screams. Flat-faced boy smashed his ears into the sides of his head, trying to stifle the shrieks with his humongous palms. They had lined every crack in the apartment with old clothes, towels, sheets— anything to keep the sorrow from leaking in.

Once inside the door of apartment 6D, the bed-headed woman tossed the day's conquest onto the barren kitchen table. The leather-bound journal rested on the tabletop as if it had always belonged there in the black linoleum desert, a seasoned expert at surviving on the droplets of water left twice a day by compulsive sponging.

Flat-faced boy opened the refrigerator and poked his head inside. Read it, he ordered to the cheese drawer.

So the bed-headed woman picked up the journal of Charlotte Cooper and read each entry out loud while the flat-faced boy boiled water for rice and opened a can of beans. A stranger's secrets and dreams felt like recently eaten chocolate on the bed-headed woman's tongue, mysterious and bittersweet. Charlotte Cooper began recording her life story on the 29th of April, 1994—the day her husband stopped loving her. The bed-headed woman silently noted the tear-stained page of August 17th, 1996. When she finished, she found a place on the shelf for Charlotte, sandwiched between the rainbow pages of Nora Channing and the black book of Tyrone Whitney.

The flat-faced boy and the bed-headed woman have yet to find a story they've never heard before.

Bed-headed woman sighed. Better luck tomorrow.

ACKNOWLEDGMENTS

Behind each piece contained in this book is a small army of individuals dedicated to empowering students through writing. They go to astonishing lengths to accomplish this: illustrating field trip stories in front of a class of exacting second graders; spending hours editing audio and film for multimedia workshops; convincing middle school students that persuasive essays can be both effective and hilarious; supportively encouraging high school students to talk about what is meaningful to them; even dressing up as zombies, complete with stage makeup, when the occasion calls for it. We feel incredibly lucky to call these people 826CHI volunteers and we are grateful for everything they do.

For their colossal help in this year's *Compendium* review process, we thank 826CHI volunteers Lori Barrett, Brad Brubaker, Carrie Colpitts, Laura Fox, Shawn Gaines, Josh Lesser, Tricia Lunt, Laura Perelman, Janet Potter, Lynne Roberts, Sean Shatto, and Kara Thorstenson. Our thanks also to Lilly Gray, Anna Green, and Dori Trimble, for spending their winter field work terms helping us undertake this review while kicking off our 2010 student programming year in style.

We are nothing short of astounded by the talent and commitment of interns Lauren Catey, Jeni Crone, Clare Hiatt, Allison Kelley, and Adam Kivel. Our sincere thanks goes to each of them for making this book possible, and for the countless other ways in which they have inspired both students and staff alike through their assistance in all 826CHI does.

For her vision, creativity, and guidance, we are grateful to our tireless and gifted designer, Mollie Edgar. Our great thanks also to Staci Davidson, for her meticulous proofreading. Thank you both for the many hours and stunning enthusiasm you contribute to all of our publications.

Joe Meno, it was an honor having you write the foreword to this book. Your engaged support means the world to all of us at 826CHI, most especially to the students, whose words

193

you have so eloquently appraised. Thank you for taking the dare.

Our profound thanks to the many teachers and families who have connected thousands of young writers with 826CHI and helped us spread the word and the excitement. With your help, the 826CHI community continues to grow.

Above all, we are grateful to the many students who have shared their writing with 826CHI. We thank you for your laughter, your depth, your curiosity, your dedication, and the ways in which you observe and imagine the world. Your words continue to amaze and inspire, and we are proud of and impressed by each of you. We can't wait to see what you write next.

MARA O'BRIEN, *Executive Director*
KAIT STEELE, *Associate Director*
PATRICK SHAFFNER, *Community Outreach Coordinator*
PAT MOHR, *Program Coordinator*
CORINNE KRITIKOS, *Operations Coordinator*

VOLUNTEERS, TUTORS, INTERNS, *and* WORKSHOP INSTRUCTORS

The suspiciously talented and remarkably generous individuals behind each and every aspect of 826CHI.

Anthony M. Abboreno
Lauren Abbott
Patrick Abbott
Alya Adamany
Alexa Adams
Carrie Adams
Janet Adamy
Tadd Adcox
Aaron Adler
Anisha Ahluwalia
Jodi Akst
Anaheed Alani
Katherine Albing
Arias Aldo
Elizabeth Alexander
Leah Allen

Leslie Allotta
Andy Alper
Carolyn Alterio
Jenna Altobelli
David Amaral
Omowale Amoin
Britte Anchor
Chelise Anderson
Ellie Anderson
Lisa Anderson
Taylor Anderson
Matt Anglen
Gina Anselmo
Beverly Applebaum
Noah Applebaum
Nathan Armstrong

Rachel Arndt
Andie Arthur
Kimberly Austin
George Baird
Assel Baitassova
Carroll Baker
Lindsay Baloun
Jennifer Barnes
Giselle Barone
Lori Barrett
Terence Barthel
Don Bartlett
Melissa Barton
Shawnee Barton
Josh Bartz
Aaron Bass

Jonathan Baude
Halle Bauer
Sara Bauer
Danielle Bauman
Nate Baumgart
Dan Baxter
Casey Bayer
Rowan Beaird
Anjali Becker
Billy Becker
James Behrens
Rebecca Behrens
Nancy Behrman
Mark Beidelman
Ian Belknap
Emily Bell

Quinnetta Bellows
Kimberly Bellware
David Ben-Arie
Frank Bentley
Adam Berg
Jillian Berger
Sherri Berger
Nicole Berland
Amy Bernstein
David Berthy
Lauren Besser
Arielle Bielak
Shanita Bigelow
Demian Birkins
Andrew Bishop
Shomari Black

WORKSHOPS

Harry Blacklock
Julie Blacklock
Emily Blaha
David Blatt
Amy Blevins
Lorne Bobren
Nicole Bock
Christy Bockheim
Allison Bogner
Kate Boisseau
Anna Bolm
Ana Bolotin
Kat Bolton
Loren Bondurant
Mark Bonus
Greg Boose
Dove Boyko
Ryan Boyle
Elizabeth Boyne
Becca Bradley
Daniel Brady
Aaron Brager
Sangini Brahmbhatt

Jennifer Brandel
Katie Brandt
Tom Bratt
Lauren Braun
Julie Braunstein
Julianne Breck
Cynthia Breckenridge
Trisha Breitlow
Lisa Brennan
Julia Brenner
Gavin Breyer
Holly Brinkman
Bailey Brittin
Will Broadway
Alyssa Brody
Megan Brody
Ben Broen
Anne Brogden
Max Brooks
Sarah Brown
Brad Brubaker
Kyle Bruck
Lena Bruncaj

Amanda Bruscino
Taylor Buck
Fritz Buerger
Robin Buerki
Erica Burgess
Adam Burke
Robin Burke
Eliza Burmster
Christian Burnham
Kate Burrows
Alexis Buryk
Mark Byrne
Dara Cahill
Jane Calayag
Greg Callozzo
Angie Calvin
Bryan Campen
Salvador Campos
Clarke Canedy
Matthew Capdevielle
Debbie Capone
Meredith Carey
Elyse Caringella

Dan Carlin
Matthew Carmichael
Erin Carpenter
Val Carpenter
Pat Carr
Sarah Carson
Sean Carson
Jenna Carusa
Shea Caruthers
Marty Casey
Linda Cassady
Laura Castellano
Ramon Castillo
Ximena Castro
Lauren Catey
Pete Cavanaugh
Stephanie Chacharon
Andrea Chadderdon
Sarah Chakrin
Sam Chavis
Mimi Cheng
Sharada Chidambaram
Crystal Choi

Ashlee Christian
Anthony Cipolla
Rachel Claff
Earl Clark
Matt Clark
Stephanie Clark
Brenden Clarke
Samantha Cleaver
Elizabeth Coady
Tyler Coates
Barbara Coe
Chrissy Cogswell-
Hyland
Gloria Cohen
Michael Cohen
Rick Cohen
Susan Cole
Kelly Coleman
Carrie Colpitts
Briana Colton
John Colucci
Amber Colvin
Nancy Conger

Caroline Conley
John Conneely
Dan Connelly
Kelly Connolly
Jesse Connuck
Margot Considine
Peggy Cook
Chris Coons
David Cooper
Lydia Cooper
Elizabeth Cooperman
Julia Copeland
Kevin Corcoran
Jennifer Cordeau
Martin Cortez
Chris Couch
Samantha Coulter
Lisa Marie Courtney
Nic Covey
Susie Cowen
Katherine Craft
Nathan Craig
Lindsay Crammond

Jason Crock
Jeni Crone
Matthew Cronin
Maliea Croy
Sheryl Curcio
Jordan Curnes
Michael Curran
Nada Cuvalo
Michael D'Agostino
Angela D'Agostinoe
Michelle Dahlenburg
Danielle Dahlin
Alison Daigle
Anne Danberg
Hali Danielson
Jeanna Darby
Shama Dardai
Lauren Date
Chris Davidson
Jared Davis
Lisa Davis
Ann Marie Dvorak De
  Morales

Marco De La Rosa
Alex de Raadt St. James
Kate DeBuys
Shauna Dee
Michelle Deiermann
Jon Deitemyer
Amy DeLorenzo
Dana Demas
Christine DeMonte
Joe Dempsey
Holly DeMuth
Rishi Desai
Laurie Desch
Meredith Desmond
Sally Deupree
Rachel Devitt
Heather DeWar
Brijeet Dhaliwal
Paul Dichter
Stephen Dierks
Molly Dillon
Joe DiRago
Mike Dobias

Laura Dockterman
Sarah Dolan
Jen Donahue
Rory Donnelly
Brandon Dorn
Jonathan Doster
Courtney Douglas
Jesse Dow
Karrie Dowling
Jonathan Doyle
Lisa Doyle
Sarah Doyle
Sarah Drake
Sylvia Drake
Emily Dresslar
Julie Drifmeyer
David Driscoll
Joe Drogos
Brendan Dry
Jill Dryer
Theresa Duffy
Zach Duffy
Conrad Duncker

Heather Dunkel
Ellen Dunn
Holly Dunsworth
David Dworin
Gunn Dwyer
David Dyer
Molly Each
Lindsay Eanet
Steve Eastwood
Sarah Ebel
Sara Edelstein
D. R. Edwards
Jason Eiben
Elia Einhorn
Thomas Einstein
Molly Ekerdt
Ali Elkin
Libby Ellis
Brooke Ellison
David Emanuel
Ilana Emer
Monica Eng
Gillian Engberg

Ian Epstein
Kristin Esch
Jeanne Ettelson
Jesse Evans
Andrea Everman
Bobby Evers
Mike Ewing
Thales Exoo
Erica Faaborg
Lisa Fairman
Molly Fannin
Laura Farina
Brianne Farley
Maureen Farley
Hailey Fasse
Nicole Faust
Mary Fay
Anna Fehsenfeld
Paul Fermin
Caitlin Ferrara
Chloe Fields
Maria Filippone
Adam Findlay

Mollie Firestone
Rachel Fischhoff
Holly Fisher
Joyce Fisher
John Flaherty
Amy Flamenbaum
Joe Fleischhacker
Katie Flores
Dyan Flores
James Flynn
Anne Ford
Sandy Forkins
Laura Forster
Maheshwary
Abby Foster
Jenna Fowler
Jodi Fox
Nora Fox
Laura Fox
Vincent Francone
Amelia Frank
Alysha Frankel
Nicole Franks

Jaime Freedman
Alex Frenkel
Sarah Frier
Andee Fromm
Katharine Fronk
Ian Fullerton
Duayne Fulton
Adam Gaeddert
LeAnn Gaines
Shawn Gaines
Lindsay Galan
Katy Gallagher
Maureen Gallagher
Terry Gallagher
Ashley Gallegos
Jessica Galli
Genevra Gallo-Bayiates
Grisel Gamboa
Nicholas Gardner
Lizzie Garnett
Kevin Garvey
Hoku Gearheard
Mike Gebel

Jennifer Gebhardt
Amy Gentry
Brian George
Jason Gerken
Megan Gerrity
Matt Getz
Samay Gheewala
Gil Gibori
Jennifer Gillespie
Diane Gillette
Ellen Gladish
Jeb Gleason-Allured
Tom Gleiber
Anne Glickman
Elizabeth Goetz
Sharyn Goldyn
Renee Goodenow
Jeff Goodman
Brad Gookins
James Gordon
Jessica Gordon
Katya Gorecki
JP Gorman

Sathya Gosselin
Mark Gotfredson
Ian Gould
Shannon Grady
Caitlin Graham
Sarah Grainer
Alison Grant
Heather Gray
Lisa Grayson
Kent Green
Abigail Greenbaum
Deborah Greenberg
Janelle Greene
Rachel Greenfield
Joe Grimberg
Nora Gross
Jason Grotto
Jess Grover
Peter Groves
Carrie Grucz
Eric Gueller
Leah Guenther
Carol Guerra

Michelle Guittar
Brian Gulotta
Saumya Gumidyala
Tran Ha
Audrey Haberman
Victoria Haddad
Theodore Hahn
Lynn Haller
Paul Halupka
Abbey Hambright
Jared Hamilton
Keegan Hankes
Colette Hannahan
Katie Hannon
Suzie Hanrahan
Kirsten Hansen
Kory Hansen
Steve Hanson
Mike Hanus
Reina Hardy
Devon Hargrove
Benjamin Harmon
Brandon Harper

Bradley Harris
Kathleen Harsy
Bobby Hart
Erica Hart
Wally Hasselburg
Briggs Hatton
Laura Hawbaker
Maysan Haydar
Helen Hazlett
Shuhan He
Charles Hebert
Laurel Hechanova
Dan Hefner
Marisa Heilman
Anna Heinemann
Steve Heisler
Brendan Hendrick
Marissa Heneghan
Aubrey Henretty
Laurie Hensley
Jennifer Herlein
Jessica Herman
Nicole Herman

Gerardo Herrera
Brendan Herrig
Lesley Hershman
Laura Hess
Clare Hiatt
Patrick Hicks
Michael Trevor Higgins
Rosemary Nottoli Higgins
Sarah Higgins
Katie Hill
Sheri Hillson
Kareem Hindi
Katheryn Hines
Kim Hines
Dan Hinkel
Emily Hippert
Jeremy Hirsch
Jason Hissong
Stephanie Hlywak
Mary Beth Hoerner
David Hoffman
Wayne Hoffman

Linda Hogan
Liza Hogan
Tim Hogan
Daniel Hollander
Amy Hollinger
Debbie Holm
Crystal Holmes
Sarah Holtkamp
Anne Holub
Julia Hon
Tess Hopey
Jerrod Howe
Dani Hoyler
Steve Hudson
Kimberly Hula
Wendy Hush
Rebecca Huval
Cathy Hwang
Jason Hyde
Annie Hynick
Anthony Iamurri
Caroline Imreibe
Allison Isaacson

Noah Isackson
Larissa Itomlenskis
Daniel Ivec
Brenna Ivey
Jeff Jablonski
Anna Jackson
Paul Jackson
Whitney Jackson
Jonathan Jacobson
Susan Jaffee
Joe Janes
Nick Janquart
Jaclyn Jansen
Anton Janulis
Abbie Jarman
Robert Jasenof
Alexandra Jasura-
Semer
Rachel Javellana
Kiley Jeffery
Jac Jemc
Andrea Jennings
Kellie Jensen

Matt Jensen
Peter Jensen
Justine Jentes
Drew Jerdan
Sarah Jersild
Cristina Jimenez
Gabi Jirasek
Jennifer Johannesen
Adam Johns
Ian Johnson
Jeff Johnson
Joan Johnson
Kevin Johnson
Melissa Johnson
Rachel Johnson
Valerie Johnson
Stephanie Jokich
Emily Jones
Katie Jones
Scott Jones
Siggy Jonsson
Jessica Joseph
Jim Joyce

Vera Junge
Sara Kagay
Melanie Kahl
Nora Kahn
Fergus Kaiser
Tamara Kaldor
Kunal Kalro
Roger Kamholz
Kari Kamin
Rachel Kamins
Gabrielle Kammerer
Brian Kane
Kyungmin Kang
Jon Kaplan
Phil Kaplan
Jason Karley
Kimya Karshenas
Kyle Kartz
Erin Kasdin
Andrea Kasprzak
Paul Kastner
LaCoya Katoe
Lara Kattan

Bonnie Katz
Jenny Kauchak
Nick Kawahara
Michelle Kaye
Bob Kazel
Clare Kealy
Erin Keane
Meghan Keedy
Michelle Keefe
Phillip Keefe
Arianne Keegan
Juliana Keeping
Cam Keitel
Maureen Kelleher
Beth Keller
Allison Kelley
Joanna Kelley
Taylor Kelley
Ami Kelly
Dan Kelly
Matt Kelly
Rob Kenagy
Anne Kenealy

Annie Kennedy
James Kennedy
Chad Kenward
Aileen Keown Vaux
Bonnie Kepplinger
Rian Kerfoot
Alison Kesler
Wesley Ketcham
Meghan Keys
Trisha Khanna
Christine Kim
Lisa Kim
Sharon Kim
Hayley Kimbrue
Kathryn King
Nicolette Kittinger
Adam Kivel
Phillip Klapperich
Katy Klassman
Julie Kleczek
Andrew Kline
Steve Klise
Katie Klocksin

Kristopher Knabe
Alicia Knapp
Jamie Knight
Sarah Knight
Ellen Knuti
Erin Koch
Felicity Kohn
Lorie Kolak
Annika Konrad
Shelly Koop
Andy Kopsa
Demetrios Korakis
Fred Koschmann
Rebecca Kosick
Kate Kraft
Sonia Kraftson
Melody Kramer
Maria Krasinski
Eric Kroh
Amy Krouse Rosenthal
Beth Kruger
Danielle Kuffler
Lindsay Kundel

Dan Kuruna
Martii Kuznicki
Jennie Kwon
Liz Ladach-Bark
Cristina Lalli
Maria Lalli
Jon Lamphere
Andrew Lampl
Melissa Lane
Matt Lang
Jessi Langsen
Joe Lanter
Kellyn Lappinga
Alison Lara
Brandi Larsen
Matt Larsen
Julie Larson
Laura Lash
Paul Lask
Michael Latham
Megan Lawler
Conrad Lawrence
Kate Lawroski

Nathan Leahy
Margaret Lebron
Ed Lee
Mark Lee
Kevin Leeds
Michael Lehman
Zoe Lehman
Alison Lehner
Katie Leimkuehler
Elizabeth Lenaghan
Anthony Lenhart
Cesar Lerma
Josh Lesser
Jessica Levco
Rachel Levi
Stephanie Levi
Gabriel Levinson
Hayley Levitan
Larissa Levitan
Grace Lewis
Hilary Lewis
Lauren Lewis
Rebecca Liddy

Kristina Lilleberg
Vicky Lim
Teresa Lin
Erica Lindberg
Lia Lindsey
John Link
Robin Linn
Jamison Linz
Mike Lipka
Erica Lipper
Kathryn Lisinicchia
Erin Little
Julia Lobo
Kevin Longstreth
Michele Lopatin
Morgan Lord
Elena Losey
Meredith Lovelace
Maura Lucking
Sarah Luczko
Stuart Luman
Rebecca Lund
Samantha Lundequam

Jessica Lunney
Tricia Lunt
Jean Luo
Annie Lydgate
Shianne Lyles
Laura Lytle
Faren MacDonald
Nikki Macey
Sandy Machugin
Chris Mack
Hisham Madani
Tanya Madison-Ogboi
Jessica Madsen
Erinrose Mager
Gabriel Magliaro
Tim Magner
Christine Magnotta
Ellen Mahon
Ben Majoy
Rohit Malhotra
Jason Malikow
Daniel Mallory
Dianne Malueg

Shaun Manning
Katie Marcuz
Rebecca Margolis
Sado Marinovic
Clay Markwell
Jenna Marotta
Jessica Marsh
Maya Marshall
Jessica Martell
Nate Martin
Alyssa Martinez
Galen Mason
Lisa Massura
Jeff Matheis
Amber Matheson
Andrew Matson
Tasha Matsumoto
Lex Mattera
Tamara Matthews
Paula Mauro
Miranda Max
Alisa Mazur
Liz Mazur

Liz McCabe
Katie McCaughan
Andrew McClain
Meghan McCook
Morgan McDonald
Margaret McEachern
Bridget McFadden
Molly McGee
Catherine McGeeney
Tom McHenry
Maureen McHugh
Becka McKay
Kerri McKeand
Erin McMahan
Sarah McMurrough
Sean McMurrough
Jessica McNaughton
Paula McNicholas
Heather McShane
Jennifer McSurley
Joy Meads
Jay Meerbaum
Rudy Mehrbani

Jordan Meinholz
Meredith Melragon
Sarah Meltzer
Jason Menard
Rob Mentzer
Sergio Mercado
Megan Mercer
Sarah Merchlewitz
Carrie Messenger
Betsy Messimer
Lynn Metz
Vaughan Meyer
Vida Mikalcius
Betsy Mikel
Naomi Millan
David Miller
Hayley Miller
Jolene Miller
Rose Miller
Rubin Miller
Lindsey Miller
Megan Milliken
Shannon Milliken

Jessica Milnaric
Max Minor
Chris Mitchell
Jane Moccia
Sally Moeller
Steve Molnar
Catherine Monahan
Kendra Monroe
Lily Mooney
Heidi Moore
Natalie Moore
Nora Moore
Paul Moore
Michael Moreci
CJ Morello
Meredith Morgan
Alyssa Morin
Sondra Morin
Nika Morley
Emily Moroni
Amanda Morris
Ryan Morris
Emily Morrison

Robin Morrissey
Jason Mortensen
Michael Mortitz
David Moskowitz
Jessie Moskowitz
John Moss
Kat Mounts
Mark Moyes
Joe Moylan
Rozanna Mroz
Corinne Mucha
Tracy Mumford
Michael Munley
Hugh Musick
Dana Muvceski
Benjamin Nadler
Sandy Naing
Nathan Nanfelt
Courtney Nash
Troy Nee
Susanne Nelsen
Blake Nelson
John Nelson

Regina Nelson
John Neurater
Hannibal Newsom
Dan Nguyen
Lance Nicholls
Kris Nielsen
Chris Niemyjski
Anne Marie Nist
Michael Nitschky
Cole Nonderee
Alexis Nordling
Rachel Notor
Tricia Nowacki
Sarah Nun
Carla Nuzzo
John O'Brien
Kim O'Connor
Amy O'Daniel
Nora O'Donnell
Brian O'Grady
Sean O'Leary
Dan O'Neil
Katie-Anne O'Neil

Katie Obriot
Amy Odenthal
Kate Ogden
Dana Oliveri
April Olsen
Chris Oposnow
Elizabeth Ordonez
Sidera Origer
Lori-May Orillo
Joey Orr
Josh Orr
Maurya Orr
Kristin Orser
Jacqueline Ostrowski
Jacob Otting
Marc Ovies
Barry Owen
Jen Page
Christopher Palafax
Jessica Palmer
Michael Palmer
Monica Palmer
Tom Palmer

Peggy Panosh
Melanie Pappadis
Liz Pardee
Daniel Park
Dustin Park
Frances Park
Trevor Park
Lisa Parker-Short
Rebecca Parker
Scott Parker
Ford Parsons
Monique Parsons
Brigid Pasulka
Krupa Patel
Bindiya Patel
Gavin Paul
Laura Pearson
Frances Peebles
Valerie Pell
Kate Pemberton
Amy Pemble
Emily Penn
Chris Penna

Laura Perelman
Brad Perkins
Becky Perlman
Rebecca Pernic
Leslie Perrine
Aisha Pervaiz
Emi Peters
Kristin Peters
Krissy Peterson
Michael Peterson
Dan Petrella
Kristen Petrillo
Conor Pewarski
Jenny Pfafflin
Ashley Pflaumer
Mary Philips
Cassie Phillips
Kelly Phillips
Joan Philo
Carli Pierce
Meagan Pierce
Erik Pierson
Brynna Pietz

Jane Piglianelli
Joi Podgorny
Claire Podulka
Susan Pogash
Anne Polick
David Pompei
Chelsea Potter
Janet Potter
Emily Power
Augie Praley
Dan Prazer
Kimberly Priebe
Tom Priebe
Kate Prockovic
Kamala Puligandla
Aparna Puppala
Rebecca Pyles
Christine Quinn
Drennen Quinn
Akasha Rabut
Heather Radke
Brian Rady
Daniel Raeburn

Nandita Raghuram
Anne Raih
Vicki Rakowski
Megha Ralapati
Amol Ray
Lucy Raymond
Mariel Razalan
Katie Reardon
Laura Reasons
Gail Reich
Rebecca Reid
Dave Reidy
Brittany Reilly
Moira Reilly
Kelly Reilly
Craig Reinbold
Breanne Reindl
Natalie Reinhart
Aaron Renier
Courtney Reynolds
Jeffery Rhodes
Julia Rice
Mary Richards

Ramona Richards
Matthew Richardson
Allison Rickard
Megan Riggle
Mandy Rinder
Jessica Ripper
Joan Ritchey
Sam Ritchey
Katja Rivera
Alice Robbins
Jesse Robbins
Jane Roberti
Lynne Roberts
Helena Robertson
Kellie Robertson
Annie Robinson
Dana Robinson
Tony Robinson
Allison Roche
Jenny Roche
Aine Rock
Kathleen Rockwell
Scott Rodd
Cristina Rodriguez

Laura Roeder
Clint Rogers
Cynthia Rogowski
Blair Rohrbach
Jennifer Rolniak
Perry Romanowski
Ellen Rosen
Ben Rosenberg
Andy Rosenstein
Christina Rosetti
Joshua Rothhaas
Adam Roubitchek
Amanda Rowe
Sumit Roy
Ben Rubenstein
Adam Rubin
Joshua Ruddy
Joanna Rudenborg
Annie Rudnik
Michele Rudoy
Amy Ruff
Alyssa Rusak
Nina Rusiecki
Peter Russell

Sara Ruzomberka
Claire Ryan
Erin Ryan
Kyle Ryan
Mike Sack
Kim Sagami
Dave Salanitro
Brian Sallade
Kelsey Salmen
Tyler Samples
Emily Sandberg
Peter Sander
Cassy Sanders
Emilie Sandoz
Elizabeth SanFilipo
Shannon Sapolich
Paige Sarlin
Cheryl Sauber
Brandy Savarse
Megan Saxelby
Kathryn Scanlan
Jennifer Schelewitz
Erika Schmidt
Cassandra Schmutz

James Schneider
Amy Schoenhals
Michael Schramm
Matt Schrecengost
Julie Schriefer
Kate Schriner
Leigh Schrock
Jason Schrowe
Timothy Schuler
Sam Schulhfer-Wohl
Kelly Schultz
Stacy Schultz
Brynn Schwaba
Erica Schwanke
Liz Scordato
Amanda Scotese
Mark Scott
Stephanie Seagle
Carly Seguin
Elizabeth Self
Shauna Seliy
Jessica Server
Romulo Severino
Paras Shah

Kashif Shaikh
Lisa Shames
Daniel Shapiro
Sean Shatto
Diane Shaughnessy
Frank Shaw
Allyson Shea
Kristin Sheehan
Emily Shepherd
Anne Shepherd
Douglas Shetterly
Sarah Morris Shultz
Merissa Shunk
Andrea Silenzi
Lia Silver
Katie Simon
Steve Simoncic
Gabrielle Sinclair
Sarah Singer
Matt Singer
Gogi Singh
Patrick Sisson
Sarah Skerrett
Maggie Skoller

Justin Skolnick
Mahrinah Slagle
Jason Sloat
Annie Slotnick
Ashley Smart
Caitlyn Smith
Claire Smith
David Smith
Derrick Smith
Jeremy Smith
Kyle Smith
Laura Smith
Nicole Smith
Sarah Smith
Troy Smothers
Anna Smunt
Amy Snickenberger
Anna Snickenberger
Marie Snyder
Lisa Soare
Kate Soderberg
Abraham Sohn
Brian Solem
Sarah Soler

Dan Solomon
Elaine Soloway
Chresten Sorensen
Kate Soto
Raquel Soto
Natalie Southwick
Marissa Spalding
Kathryn Spangler
Kevin Sparrow
Cecilia Sperry
Jed Spiegelman
Michelle Springer
Caitlin Stainken
Justin Staley
Elizabeth Stamberger
Kati Stanford
Lesley Stanley
Jennifer Statler
Peter Steadman
Meg Steele
Camilla Stefl
Amelia Stegall
Emily Rose Stein
Noah Stein

Julia Steinberger
Sierra Sterling
Natalie Sternberg
Smith Steve
Alice Stevens
John Stevens
Katie Stevens
Dana Stewart
Wendy Stewart
Juell Stewart
Chris Stiles
Sarah Stoehr
Wes Stokes
Ellen Stolar
Laryssa Stolarskyj
Rachel Stone
Jon Stookey
Scarlett Stoppa
Jen Strauss
Brenna Stuart
Matt Sudman
John Suh
Cayenne Sullivan
Karen Sullivan

Marin Sullivan
Shirley Sung
Chamberlin Susan
Mark Sussman
Allison Swade
Beth Swierczewski
T.J. Szafranski
Mark Szczuka
Ryan Tacata
Daniel Tafelski
Sheera Talpaz
Anna Marie Tamayo
Laura Tan
Bill Tanner
Diane Taviner
Sally Taylor
Patty Templeton
Allison Tenn
John Theisen
Karen Thimell
Matthew Thom
Andrea Thomalla
Alexis Thomas
Annie Thompson

Ryan Thompson
Kara Thorstenson
Kate Tkacik
Melissa Tobler
Cameron Todd
Adam Torres
Nicole Trafton
Vy Tran
Adam Travis
Jeffrey Treem
Le Trieu
Louise Tripp
Lisa Trudeau
Jennifer Tsang
Gwen Tulin
Peter Tulloch
Melissa Turner
Susan Twetten
Kate Udovicic
Holly Ulasovich
Bora Un
David Unger
Daniel Usellis
Karen Uselmann

Liz Vadas
Lila Valinoti
Whitney Van Arsdall
Stein Van Der Ploeg
Jon Van Hofwegen
Paul Van Slembrouck
Eric VanDemark
Mark Vanderhoff
Allison Vanek
Kylie Vanerstrom
Jaida Vaught
Asha Veal
Liliana Velazquez
Paula Velde
Brittany Verrette
Jennifer Verson
Matt Vester
JoLynn Villaro
Terin Vintizil
Evan Voboril
Erin Vogel
Mary Volk
Sera Vorpahl
Chris Wachal

Gretchen Wahl
Mike Wakcher
Libby Walker
Ted Walker
Chelsea Lane Walls
Molly Walsh
Erin Walter
Matt Walter
Rebecca Walz
Elizabeth Wampler
Steven Warmbir
Alyson Paige Warren
Sarah Beth Warshauer
Anna Washenko
Jessica Wasserman
Rachel Watson
Nicky Way
Alex Wayman
Erik Weber
Sally Weigel
Heather Weiler
Kate Weinberg
Matthew Weingast

Lindsey Weis
Tracy Weisman
Jeremy Weiss
Greg Weissel
Sandor Weisz
Tyler Wellington
Zoe Wendel
Sarah Werner
Tomasz Werner
Winter Werner
Joshua Westlund
Lauren Wetherbee
Patty Wetli
Aaron White
Ana White
Bryan White
Henry White
Natalie White
Cate White
Thomas Whittington
Jessica Wigent
Crystal Williams
Ryan Williams
Stephanie Williams

Karl Williamson
John Wilmes
Anna Wilson
Colleen Wilson
Jeremy T. Wilson
Kea Wilson
Lauren Wilson
Lisa Wilson
Ryan Wilson
Stefanie Wilson
Elizabeth Winkowski
Emily Winter
Anne Wirtz
Max Wise
Ryan Witthans
Jennifer Wojciechowski
Jacy Wojcik
David Wolinsky
Tracy Woodley
Tanisha Woodson-Shelby
Renee Woodward
Patrick Woyna
Mars Wright

Peter Wright
Carolyn Wrobel
Beth Wydler
Holly Wysel
Diana Xin
Michelle Yacht
Diane Yamazaki
Dave Yang
Prathima Yeddanapudi
Lena Yohey
Sarah Yoo
Laura Young
Emily Youseff
Lauren Yurman
Haifa Zabout
Christina Zambon
Jan Zasowski
Jay Zawadzki
Sam Zelitch
Nicole Zillmer
Yvonne Zusel
Dina Zwiebel

WORKSHOP DESCRIPTIONS

A 'Whole' Lot of Food and Memoir Writing

TAUGHT BY *Scarlett Stoppa*
Grades 4–8 | Fall 2009

How would you describe an olive? Is it salty and surprising? Does it taste like the ocean? Or does it remind you of your grandpa, who eats them exclusively for lunch? In this workshop, students met at Whole Foods Market to sample a variety of interesting fare while working on descriptive writing skills. After exploring the finer points of food writing, the group wrote short memoirs about their own experiences with a favorite meal made with family. Students shared their pieces on Whole Foods' stage before friends, family, and foodies at large.

Elementary Writing Camp I

TAUGHT BY *826CHI Staff and Interns*
Grades 2–4 | Summer 2009

This perennial session brought students to 826CHI for an assortment of high-energy writing activities. Whether writing about high-seas adventures or assuming superhero personae, students continued to develop new skills and refine old ones over the summer. A particular favorite during the workshop was Poetry Day, where students explored a variety of poetic forms, including the ever-popular 5W's poem.

I Was a Teenage Zine Fiend: A Zine Writing Workshop

TAUGHT BY *Jim Joyce and Carrie Colpitts*
Grades 7–12 | Fall 2009

So let's get this straight—you love writing, but you can't figure out how to get people to read it? You're a budding artist/sketcher/painter/margin-doodler, but you're not sure what to do with your work? You love music and want to share your love with others? We've got one word for you: ZINE. In this workshop, students explored the world of self-published magazines and set about creating their own. A month-long bonanza of writing, reading, crafting, listening to music, and general pizza-fueled creativity resulted in a class zine filled with fiction, poetry, and the occasional manifesto.

Middle School Writing Camp II

TAUGHT BY *826CHI Staff and Interns*
Grades 5–8 | Summer 2009

This summer session of writing activities included everything from poetry to music reviews to off-the-wall character sketches. One of the most popular activities was small group story making, in which we asked students to write and illustrate their own children's books for younger students.

Newsbreak Breakout!

TAUGHT BY *Larissa Itomlenskis*
Grades 3–5 | Fall 2009

210

If you could interview anyone, from anywhere, who (or what) would you choose? Your subject might be real or imaginary, from the past or from the future. With the right questions, everything's got a story. In this workshop, students explored the role of both TV journalist and interviewee as they dreamt up an ideal interview subject—which ultimately included everything from Moby Dick to a glue stick—and wrote their own news program scripts.

Poemography

TAUGHT BY *Zach Duffy*

Grades 4–8 | Fall 2009

What is "Poemography" you ask? As hybrids go, it's as cool as a liger. Poemography is the advanced art of writing poems based on photography. It might be a haiku inspired by a picture of the Chicago El or a sonnet based on a photograph of your best friend. In this workshop, students learned about the basics of photography and explored the neighborhood with disposable cameras. After capturing their inspiration on film, students used their photographs as fodder for a book of poetry.

Salt Water + You = Art Making + Haiku

TAUGHT BY *Meghan McCook*

Grades 3–8 | Spring 2009

Taught in collaboration with the David Weinberg Gallery by artist and Education Program Director Meghan McCook, students learned about the body of work, *Salt Water* by Jennifer Scott McLaughlin. McLaughlin uses ideas and imagery from nature to create whimsical mixed media paintings depicting colorful nature scenes and organic forms. Hosted both at the gallery and at 826CHI, students used McLaughlin's work as inspiration to create an original multi-media piece of artwork using real plants and flowers, and wrote haiku poetry to accompany their creations.

Sir Downward Dog and the Goddess of Cobraland Unite under a Dancing Half-Moon: Yoga! Storytelling! Illustrating!

TAUGHT BY *Colette Hannahan*

Grades 4–8 | Fall 2009

This workshop brought together young yogis, yoginis, and the moderately flexible to discover the world of yoga. Students learned basic practices and terminology and set about inspiring their minds through breath and movement. With creative juices in perfect balance, the group created a book of 'Vinyasa fables' based on the names of their freshly-learned poses.

Travel the World Through Chocolate

TAUGHT BY *Katy Klassman and Gabrielle Kammerer*

Grades 4–8 | Spring 2009

Did you know you can travel the world without ever leaving home? All you need is a little cocoa and a lot of imagination. Under the expert instruction of workshop instructors from Vosges Haut-Chocolat, students explored new landscapes, cultures, and people through the world of chocolate. Those involved in this sweet adventure learned about the history of chocolate, how to make chocolate (watch out for the Oreo-and-curry powder combination), and the proper way to eat chocolate, before writing a how-to guidebook for others.

212

Young Writers Camp with Local Authors

TAUGHT BY *826CHI Staff and a Bunch of Literary Geniuses*
Grades 8–12 | Summer 2009

During the Young Writers Camp, we welcomed a group of intrepid students to a weeklong extravaganza at and around 826CHI. Over the course of this literary marathon, students set out to create a chapbook inspired by the writing and words of an all-star lineup of visiting writers and artists. Our guest teachers for the week included Elizabeth Crane, Monica Eng, Tran Ha, Alex Kotlowitz, Joe Meno, Aaron Renier, Robbie Q. Telfer, Rachel Webster, and Sam Weller.

213

ABOUT 826CHI

826CHI is a non-profit organization dedicated to supporting students ages 6 to 18 with their creative and expository writing skills, and to helping teachers inspire their students to write. Our services are structured around the understanding that great leaps in learning can happen with one-on-one attention, and that strong writing skills are fundamental to future success.

826CHI provides after-school tutoring, class field trips, writing workshops, and in-schools programs—all free of charge—for students, classes, and schools. All of our programs are challenging and enjoyable, and ultimately strengthen each student's power to express ideas effectively, creatively, confidently, and in his or her individual voice.

826CHI is one of eight chapters of 826 National, a non-profit tutoring, writing, and publishing organization with locations in eight cities across the country. 826 Valencia, the flagship center in San Francisco, was founded by writer/editor Dave Eggers and educator Nínive Calegari in 2002. 826CHI opened its doors to Chicago students in October of 2005, joining 826 Valencia, 826LA, 826NYC, 826 Seattle, and 826michigan. In 2007, 826 Boston also joined our national network of 826 chapters. This year, we are excited to welcome 826DC as the most recent addition to the 826 family.

OUR PROGRAMS

826CHI's free programs reach students at every opportunity—in school, after school, in the evenings, and on weekends.

After-School Tutoring and Writing

826CHI's site is packed four afternoons a week with students who come in for free one-on-one tutoring after school. We serve students of all skill levels and interests, most of whom live or go to school within walking distance of our writing center. Literacy is stressed through daily reading and daily projects at the Writing Table, as well as monthly chapbook projects, where students' writing around a particular theme is compiled into small books and shared at family and community readings. Pre-registration is not required, and students are welcome to show up any school day, Monday through Thursday, from 3 until 5:30PM.

Field Trips

We want to help teachers get their students excited about writing while also helping students better express their ideas. 826CHI invites teachers to bring their students to our site for high-energy field trips during the school days. Teachers may choose from several field trip formats depending on their interests and grade level. A group of tutors is also on-hand during every field trip, whether we are helping to generate new material or to revise already written work. The field trip program is so popular that our schedule is consistently filled almost a year in advance. To join our educator e-mail list to be notified when our registration for the next school year opens, please visit our website at:

www.826chi.org.

In-Schools

At a teacher's behest, we will send tutors into classrooms around the city to provide one-on-one assistance to students as they tackle various projects—Young Authors books, research papers, journalism projects, literary magazines, basic writing assignments, and college entrance essays. If you are a teacher interested in inviting our tutors into your classroom, please contact us through our website.

Workshops

826CHI offers free workshops that provide in-depth writing instruction in a variety of areas that schools often cannot include in their curriculum, such as college entrance essay writing, bookmaking, journalism, comic book making, playwriting, and songwriting. These innovative workshops allow students to hone and advance their skills while having fun and developing a greater sense of the joy of writing. All workshops are project-based and are taught by experienced, accomplished professionals and volunteers. Connecting Chicago students with these creative and generous mentors allows students to dream and achieve on a grand scale. Please visit our website to view our current workshop schedule.

Student Publishing

At 826CHI, we know the quality of student work is greatly enhanced when it is shared with an authentic audience. All of our activities are project-based, whether they result in an end-of-project book, a class performance, a gallery exhibit, a short film, or an exceptionally rockin' CD. As a writing center, we are especially committed to publishing student work for students to share with their friends, family, the public at-large, and the entire universe. Student publications may take the form of small chapbooks that we bind in-house or in professionally published volumes, such as this one. All forms of student publishing are available for purchase through The Boring Store.

THE BORING STORE

826CHI shares its space with The Boring Store, Chicago's only undercover secret agent supply store. The Boring Store offers spy supplies in a highly-secretive way. We have grappling hooks, envelope x-ray spray, pigeon oil (if your carrier pigeon lacks luster), and an ever-expanding array of fake moustaches. Proceeds from The Boring Store go directly toward supporting 826CHI's programs for Chicago students. Can't risk being tailed by enemy agents? Have no fear. You can also conduct your highly classified operations online at: **www.notasecretagentstore.com**.

Please visit us online at www.826chi.org or in-person at 1331 North Milwaukee Avenue in the Wicker Park neighborhood of Chicago to learn more about our programs and to find out how you can get involved.